Project Planning
Techniques

Project Planning Techniques

Parviz F. Rad, PhD, PE, CCE, PMP

Vittal S. Anantatmula, DSc, CCE

𝄞 MANAGEMENTCONCEPTS

𝄢
MANAGEMENTCONCEPTS
8230 Leesburg Pike, Suite 800
Vienna, VA 22182
(703) 790-9595
Fax: (703) 790-1371
www.managementconcepts.com

Printed in the United States of America

Library of Congress Cataloging-in-Publication Data

Rad, Parviz F., 1942–
    Project planning techniques/Parviz F. Rad, Vittal S. Anantatmula.
        p. cm.
    Includes bibliographical references and index.
    ISBN 1-56726-165-5 (pbk.)
    1. Project management. 2. Cost control. I. Anantatmula, Vittal S., 1955–
    II. Title.

HD69.P75P335 2005
658.4'012—dc22

                                                                    2005049565

Chapter 2 is an adaptation of a paper by Parviz F. Rad, "Advocating a Deliverable-Oriented Work Breakdown Structure," that was originally published by AACE International in *Cost Engineering*, Volume 41, Issue 12, December 1999. Reprinted with the permission of AACE International, 209 Prairie Ave., Suite 100, Morgantown, WV 25601, USA. Phone 800-858-COST/304-296-8444. Fax: 304-291-5728. Internet: http://www.aacei.org. E-mail: info@aacei.org. Copyright © by AACE International; all rights reserved.

About the Authors

Parviz F. Rad, PhD, PE, CCE, PMP, is an independent project management consultant. He holds an MSc from Ohio State University and a PhD from Massachusetts Institute of Technology. He has over 35 years of professional experience, during which he has served in governmental, industrial, and academic capacities. He has participated in project management activities and in the development and enhancement of quantitative tools in project management in a multitude of disciplines, including software development, construction, and pharmaceutical research. He has authored and coauthored more than 60 publications in the areas of engineering and project management. Dr. Rad is the past Editor of the *Project Management Journal.*

Vittal S. Anantatmula, DSc, CCE, is the director of the graduate degree program in project management, School of Business, The George Washington University. He has more than eight years of academic experience in research, teaching, and administration. Dr. Anantatmula previously worked in the petroleum and power industries as an electrical engineer and project manager. As a consultant, he worked with the World Bank, Arthur Andersen, and other private international consulting firms. He has authored numerous publications and has been an invited speaker at several conferences and meetings. Dr. Anantatmula is a certified cost engineer and his academic qualifications include Doctor of Science in engineering management from The George Washington University, MS (Engineering Management), MBA, and BE in Electrical Engineering.

To my son Javan

PFR

To my wife Manga

VSA

Table of Contents

Preface

We were motivated by two factors to write this book. The first is that many of the currently available books dealing with project planning cover the subject in a discipline-specific mode, such as construction planning and management, software development planning, and process plant planning and scheduling. Admittedly, there is a great deal of commonality in project planning—and ultimately project management—techniques across all industries. However, distilling the non-discipline-specific topics is sometimes difficult because they tend to get masked by the details of the discipline that is the subject of the project.

The second factor that motivated us to write *Project Planning Techniques* is our belief in the need for a book that reflects a balance of both practical experience and academic rigor in project management. Our years of experience managing projects in industry and teaching project management in university settings have convinced us of the need for a catalyst for project management professionals to develop a deeper understanding of the subject matters from this dual professional and academic perspective.

In this book, we cover the fundamentals of project planning in a discipline-independent context. We provide a quick overview of project planning, estimating, scheduling, progress monitoring, change management, and knowledge management. We direct particular attention to the accuracy of the estimates for cost and duration, as well as the issues surrounding cost and schedule overruns.

The introductory chapter deals with project selection and prioritization with the use of indices and models. Chapters 2 and 3 describe in some detail the processes and intricacies involved in developing a work breakdown structure (WBS) and a resource breakdown structure (RBS). These chapters delineate the steps involved in constructing the WBS and the RBS, which are the fundamentals of a good project plan and which provide a logical basis for project monitoring and control. Examples of WBS and RBS are provided at the ends of these chapters.

Chapter 4 introduces the concept of bottom-up estimating and the steps involved in creating a detailed estimate baseline. It also discusses the various models that estimators use to arrive at rough estimates during the early stages of project conception. The chapter discusses the issues of estimate accuracy and baseline volatility in the context of the need to provide estimates for use in making judgments about project authorization.

Chapter 5 deals with developing the schedule network and, ultimately, the project schedule. This chapter emphasizes the importance of cost and schedule integration. Chapter 6 addresses project planning and project management issues as they relate to external projects. The topics of bidding, specifications, indirect cost, and overhead are discussed, particularly as they relate to contractor performance and how it affects the client-contractor relationship.

Chapter 7 deals with the processes and techniques involved in monitoring project resource expenditures during the project implementation phase. Chapter 8 shows how the data collected by the monitoring activities will assist the project manager in dealing with the inevitable changes that occur during project implementation. It also covers the causes of changes to the project environment and the procedures involved in resolving problems that arise from these unexpected changes.

Finally, Chapter 9 addresses the emerging concept of the relationship and similarities between knowledge management and project management, stressing the importance of managing project knowledge by integrating project management and knowledge management systems.

With the hope that *Project Planning Techniques* will serve as a complete reference, we also have included a CD containing a set of comprehensive examples, including RBS, WBS, project estimates, and network diagrams, that represent several different industries.

Parviz F. Rad

Vittal S. Anantatmula

Acknowledgments

The authors would like to thank Dr. Denis F. Cioffi for co-authoring the original draft of Chapters 3 and 4 of this book. The authors would also like to thank the many students of Mgt270 at The George Washington University who provided the inspiration and practical examples for this book. Specifically, the authors would like to thank the students whose coursework has become the examples of this book.

1 Introduction

Project planning is the art and science of using the historical data, archived information, personal expertise, institutional memory, organizational knowledge, and project scope statement to predict a project's resource expenditures, total cost, and duration. Project planning also includes developing guidelines for ensuring the quality of the deliverable, responding to adverse events, and dealing with the inevitable changes to the project plan.

To arrive at an estimate of the project's cost and duration, the project manager will identify the various constituent physical elements and related activities that are necessary to meet the project's objectives. Based on this information, the project manager will estimate the amount of resources and length of time necessary for each of the constituent elements of the project.

The estimate of the cost starts with the estimate of resources, which is more valuable to the project team. Then the resource estimate is reduced to cost, because total cost usually is more important to the client. The project manager then develops the estimate by summing the estimate of resources for these elements. Next, the project manager computes the elemental cost and the total cost for the project. He or she develops a schedule network depicting the sequential relationships between the project elements. Then, using this network, the project manager calculates the project duration.

The information necessary for a comprehensive and accurate set of plans includes details of the objective, scope, quality, and delivery date. When the project is conceived, the first estimates of cost and duration are inaccurate because very little information is available about the expected deliverables, the project team, and the project environment. As the project evolves and more information becomes available, the estimate can be fine-tuned.

The evolving planning documents also might include increasing details about the procedures that will be used when implementing the project. Thus, the project plans should be updated frequently, even if there are no changes in scope. Additionally, changes in project plans might become necessary because of expanded or modified client requirements, environmental changes, and changes in design philosophy.

To develop a detailed and logical set of estimates for cost and schedule, two separate structures must be created, defined, or modified for the purposes of a project: the work breakdown structure (WBS) and the resource breakdown structure (RBS). Successful project management depends on a well-defined and fully implemented WBS and RBS. With such comprehensive tools in hand, a successful project can be achieved through clear planning, accurate reporting, and regular updating. As project details become available, they will trigger enhancements to the WBS, RBS, estimate, schedule, and other project planning documents.

The estimates of the cost and duration of the WBS elements and the project that are developed during the early stages of the project will form the baseline budget for measuring its cost and schedule performance during the implementation phase. The cost estimate, and hence the budget, will initially be very rough and inaccurate, as is the anticipated delivery date.

When establishing the project budget on the basis of the project estimate, the project manager must keep in mind whether the estimate was developed using a rough conceptual estimate technique or a detailed bottom-up estimate. If the budget was established in the early stages of planning, it will be less accurate. The budget development process, therefore, should be open to modification. In enlightened organizations, the project budget will go through continued enhancements as the details of the project are being developed.

During budget development, awareness of the degree of the baseline estimate's accuracy is essential when making commitments for time and cost and when comparing projects. Similarly, when making judgments regarding variances during the project progress monitoring phase, knowing the accuracy of the baseline is critical. During the implementation phase, the project estimates of cost and delivery date will serve as the basis for developing quantitative indicators of the project's performance.

The estimate of cost and duration, which forms the baseline for progress monitoring, should be vigorously updated during the entire lifecycle of the project, and particularly during its early stages. Depending on the accuracy and limitations of the estimate, the project manager should incorporate appropriate contingencies, reserves, and flexibilities into the budget so that at any point it is realistic and accurate.

The credibility, accuracy, and completeness of the project plans will be enhanced by the project manager's skills in disciplines related to the project, such as engineering, technology, information systems, manufacturing, assembly, marketing, management, or production planning. The project manager's expertise must extend into the areas of business, management, finance, and all facets of project management activities.

It is unrealistic to expect one person to have expertise in all of these areas, so organizations sometimes form planning committees or planning boards. The members of these boards come from all disciplines affected by the project, such as IT, engineering, operations, business development, purchasing, contracting, financial management, and of course the project team and representatives from the project management office.

The project's cost estimate is derived by adding the resource expenditure, and hence the cost, of the project's individual components. The estimate duration also is derived from WBS elements—not in a linear summary fashion, but rather from calculations of a schedule network. With the expectation that cost estimating and scheduling processes use the same structural foundation, the estimate of the duration of the project's component elements is used in developing the schedule network, which in turn will formulate a time management structure for the project.

Thus, the relationship between the cost and the schedule of the project is interdependent. The project manager should keep this interdependence in mind during project implementation, when the changes in scope and specifications cause changes in project cost or schedule. The relationship between cost and schedule must continually be reviewed as the project evolves, when detailed project plans are formulated, when more definitive baselines are established, and finally when the inevitable tradeoffs must be made during the implementation phase.

A review of marginal or failed projects shows that the vast majority of them suffered from lack of detailed planning, or that the procedures for managing were casual and ad-hoc. Conversely, the literature shows that organizations that encourage detailed planning experience far better financial growth compared to those organizations that do not. Finally, organizations that employ competent project management professionals and consistent project management procedures tend to produce more successful projects (Ibbs & Kwak 1997; Vigder & Kark 1994).

When the project is in its formative stages, very little information about it is available. Consequently, the accuracy and dependability of the estimate are very low. In other words, the risks of unforeseen and undesirable occurrences in the project are very high. Therefore, early plans and budgets are usually far from definitive, and they rarely predict the actual cost of individual components and the definitive cost of the total project.

During the early stages of the project, modifications to project plans can be formulated and conducted with minimal impact on cost and schedule. As the project proceeds, the cost of implementing modifications to the baseline plan increases substantially, although the risk and possibility of such events is lower at that point.

The bottom-up estimate uses a detailed WBS and RBS and is preferred over the less accurate and less sophisticated methods. Creating these structures requires nominal time and effort. However, for the purposes of project initiation and the project charter, and in the absence of sufficient information, rough estimates will be used during the early stages of the project.

PROJECT SCOPE AND OBJECTIVES

The client's needs and preferences are communicated to the project team through such documents as the project charter, project objectives, project scope statement, and project specifications. The terms "requirements," "specifications," and "scope" are often used interchangeably, and sometimes differently, depending on the industry of the project. Construction, industrial, and process projects refer to the description of the deliverable as scope and specifications. Scope refers to a broader expression of the client's objectives, while specifications refers to the detailed expression of the client's objectives.

Systems and software development projects often do not use the terms "specifications" or "scope" to refer to the deliverables. Instead, they use the term "requirements" to describe the performance attributes of the projects, such as processing speed, error rate, database size, and the degree of friendliness of the deliverables.

Sometimes systems and software projects use the term "specifications" to describe the attributes of the hardware. Hardware specifications for systems and software development projects might be either predetermined by the client as part of project objectives or developed by the project team as one of the deliverable components of the project. Generally speaking, although requirements are the client's preferences that will result in the scope and quality of the deliverable, requirements and scope are not the same. The former describes the preferences and needs of the client, while the latter describes the project team's solutions in response to those needs.

The requirements document includes the client's wants and needs, the distinction being that "wants" are those items that would be nice to have, although they are not crucial to the success of the project, while "needs" are those items that are essential to the success and usability of the project deliverable. Again, this information might be very sketchy during the early stages of project evolution, and it will be refined, clarified, and progressively elaborated as more information becomes available to the client and to the project team. At some point, both sets of wants and needs should converge on a set of definitive project scope specifications documents.

Project specifications usually are included in the contract documents if the project is an external project, and particularly if the contract is awarded on a lump-sum basis. (When the client directs the activities of the project, the description of tools and techniques that the team should use in implementing the project also will be included in the specifications document.) However, enlightened organizations develop specifications documents even for their internal projects. The project objectives or specifications of an internal project usually are spelled out in an authorization memo that has the same elements as the project charter, which empowers the project manager to implement the project.

The rationale for using a project charter for an internal project is that, although an internal project does not involve a formal contract, it should have a well-defined set of objectives for scope and quality so that delivery performance can be carefully and more realistically monitored. If there are no focused project objectives, and hence no detailed specifications, the evaluation and monitoring of the internal project will become ad-hoc, inaccurate, and somewhat arbitrary.

Planning details will be initially formalized and embodied in the project charter. A typical project charter will outline the attributes of a new physical deliverable, the details of performance enhancements to a system, or the purpose of a specific service. The specific service, which is described in the project objectives, will meet the needs of the organizational objectives that will form the business case for the project. The project charter will also include any assumptions and constraints. The definition of project objectives, as reflected in the project charter, involves detailing the project scope, attributes of the deliverables, acceptance tests, scheduled delivery date, expected budget, and team structure.

A carefully drafted project charter is essential to the success of the project because the charter is the focal point and the definitive reference for managing the project's triple constraints of cost, schedule, and scope during the implementation phase. Project processes and procedures must include instructions on how to treat the project charter as a living document, to be enhanced continually. Project management procedures also must highlight uniform and consistent guidelines for developing and making modifications to the baseline project charter and its corresponding specifications.

The current version of this document will serve as a base of performance reference throughout the life of the project. Likewise, there must be procedures for drafting and continually enhancing the document that highlights the business need to which this project responds; this document is often called the business case document.

It would be highly useful if the first estimate of the cost and duration of the project were a pristine one, reflecting the optimal use of resources in crafting the deliverable. The pristine plan would be unencumbered by milestone constraints and low resource availability. Thus, it would be poised to deliver the project in the most efficient and cost-effective manner. If, however, the estimate of cost or delivery date is different from the client needs for those values, then a tradeoff analysis must be performed before the project starts. In other words, if the initial unconstrained project schedule calculations result in a date later than what the client wants, then the schedule must be compressed to comply. Likewise, if the pristine project estimate calculations result in a higher cost than reflected in the current budget, then either the scope or the schedule must be modified to bring the cost within the client's budget.

In some organizations, there might be a scarcity of resources, particularly human resources. In these cases, the project duration must be extended so that the resource demand does not exceed the level of available resources. In rare cases, the client's cost expectations are higher than the project team's estimate, and the client's delivery constraint is later than the delivery date calculated by the team. In these cases, the project team will have the rare opportunity to inform the client that they will surpass their expectations.

Sometimes the quality of the project deliverable is not explicitly addressed as one of the project objectives. Ironically, it is this issue of quality, independent of the volume of deliverables, that determines the usability of the project deliverable and the resulting satisfaction of the stakeholders.

As the client's expectations of the project results become finalized, the acceptance procedures and validation tests determine the physical quality and performance tolerances of the deliverable. Therefore, the tests must reflect all of the important operational facets of the project deliverable and not frivolous features.

In the same vein, the project team should make every effort to craft the deliverable to the spirit, and not necessarily to the letter, of these tests, which might miss some important facet of the product. This kind of due diligence on the part of the project team will promote long-term client satisfaction, which is considered one of the most important indicators of a project's success. For the purposes of this book, quality and scope are treated collectively.

The desired delivery date is the most important date in the project schedule. For a variety of historical and operational reasons, several intermediate milestones usually are defined as well. Intermediate milestones are not crucial to the execution of the project, although achieving these milestones often signifies or verifies the expected pace of the project and the desired quality of the deliverables.

Establishment of the intermediate milestones can be in response to the needs and desires of the client, the collective project team, individual team members, or the stakeholders. Establishing and monitoring the intermediate milestones provide a means of assuring the stakeholders that the project is progressing satisfactorily.

Project planning documents must include details of processes, procedures, and methodologies that will be used for monitoring the effectiveness and efficiency of the project team in producing the project deliverable. Since the project team's characteristics can have subtle but significant impacts on the project's success, the characteristics of the project team must be outlined as part of the process of planning the physical deliverable of the project. Such attributes might be the skills of team members, the administrative affiliation of team members, and the extent to which these professionals might be diverted to other duties during the time that they are involved in the project.

Project management activities that deal with team formation and the team charter must also be well defined and planned during the very early stages of the project. Finally, when the client specifies the means and modes by which the project will be conducted, the project charter and WBS might spell out the major items of equipment that will be used to craft the project deliverables and the tools that will be used to test their important attributes.

PROJECT BUSINESS CASE

Projects usually are undertaken in response to a set of goals for achieving organizational objectives. The most common categories of organizational objectives for internal projects are operating necessity, competitive necessity, or innovative ventures. Therefore, as a prelude to project selection and initiation, organizational priorities must be clearly identified and clarified, particularly as they relate to the project's utility.

One of the important components of a project charter is the statement of how the project investment is reconciled with organizational strategic goals and investment policies. Further, a detailed and clear project charter, which includes a focused business purpose and a specific objective, will enable the team to develop alternative options for achieving the same organizational goal, using innovative and creative processes in crafting the project deliverable.

The alternative projects that respond to the same opportunity must be highlighted in terms of expected deliverables, conceptual estimate, preliminary schedule, and a quantified list of benefits and risks. The plan for each project should provide the details of all of the costs, benefits, and risks associated with providing the deliverable. Accordingly, the cost and duration of each project will be considered when determining whether the project should be funded for implementation.

To reconcile the project costs with corporate investment strategies, each project must have a business objective that is aligned with the strategic plan and that will serve as the foundation for the project's investment proposal. The document containing the project objectives and investment strategies is called a business case or a business plan. It provides ample information on the project deliverable's utility. The business plan must provide a detailed description of the problem, need, or opportunity to which the project is expected to respond.

The planning documents for each project must include as much detail as possible on the project's sponsor, objectives, and deadline. The project's business plan must clearly articulate the reasons for initiating this project and the expected benefits of the project's deliverable. To satisfy this requirement, the benefits the deliverable will bring to the enterprise must be identified in the project charter or its supporting documents.

In many ways, particularly for internal projects, implicit or explicit corporate support for the project will determine its organizational viability and importance. If none of the members of senior management is willing to sponsor the project, it does not have sufficient administrative support. A formal survey of the key executives and major stakeholders sponsoring the project, therefore, must be conducted before authorizing it.

PROJECT INITIATION

In some cases, the business plan for a specific organizational objective might be related to several alternative projects. These projects might offer slightly different deliverables, and yet they all would achieve the same general business objectives. On the other hand, in some cases, one project might affect two separate organizational strategies.

In a proactive and dynamic organization, having a large portfolio of possible projects is a normal occurrence. However, funding limitations usually preclude implementing all of these projects. A formalized project ranking and selection process therefore must be developed to identify the projects with the greatest potential impact on the current organizational needs, at the lowest possible funding, and with optimized values of other issues that are important to the organization.

Selection of projects for implementation must take into consideration the organization's corporate strategic plans, realistic expectations for sophistication of the deliverables, predicted success attributes of the project, and constraints to the project's success. To make consistent and logical decisions in prioritizing the projects and selecting projects from a potentially continuous stream of options, a company-specific process of evaluating projects must be established. Finally, a project should be considered for authorization in light of the current workload of individuals, operational obligations of divisions, and financial obligations of the parent organization.

Ranking projects for implementation is most commonly conducted using an index, sometimes called a metric, or a group of indices called a model. In general, models are easy-to-use characterizations of operations, organizations, and relationships. Even the very sophisticated models, however, are only a partial representation of the reality that they attempt to portray. Further, although models are very useful as an aid in the decision-making process, they do not fully duplicate all facets of the real world. Nevertheless, models can be exploited to purge extraneous elements of a problem and to highlight the important elements of the issues surrounding the project's implementation.

The objective of the project selection process, and its accompanying model, is to rank the projects in order of the best interests of the organization. Thus, the selection process would utilize a model that is specifically formulated to optimize parameters such as organizational goals, project cost, project duration, and the anticipated attributes of the project deliverable. Depending on the organization, project selection models range from the very simple to the very complex.

Because project planning models depend on numeric input from the indices describing the characteristics of the organization and those of the project deliverable, even subjective indices ultimately must be quantified. Accordingly, the project initiation process will be refined if the quantification of the subjective model indices is based on consistent and organization-specific procedures. Then, using the project data, organizational priorities, the customized model, and the consistent scoring process, the prospective projects will be ranked systematically and in a formalized fashion.

For external projects, the number of subcontractors and the overall contracting strategy must be carefully evaluated in light of the best interests of the project and its business plan, and not simply on the basis of the lowest initial cost. Contracting strategy will affect the communication pattern among project stakeholders, and it will subtly affect project performance. The fee structure of a contractor can profoundly affect the total project cost. Therefore, a careful analysis of direct and indirect costs, overhead, and profit margin of the contractor is advisable, particularly if the contract is being awarded on a cost-plus basis.

The numerical results of the project selection model always must be tempered by the experience and professional expertise of the organizational entity that is charged with managing the project portfolio. Ideally, this entity is the Project Management Office, although the function might be performed by an ad-hoc, or standing, team designated by upper management. The project selection group is expected to make a judgment on the project's viability using the information generated by the model, although sometimes the quantified values provided by the less sophisticated models are enhanced and modified in light of the limitations and constraints of the model and its constituent indices.

Two separate sets of indices are used for the project selection process: organizational priorities and project attributes. The models that characterize the selection process include the important indices, describing these two sets of issues organized so that a quantified ranking for each project results. During a typical project selection process, one would identify organizational priorities for all projects and formulate company-specific scoring schemas for the ranking process. Thus, one can establish metrics that evaluate a specific project in the light of these priorities. A project selection model is, or should be, very organization-specific, and as such it should use a customized combination of indices to satisfy the organizational project selection objectives.

The indices used for project selection tend to fall into two major categories. Figures 1-1 and 1-2 show a listing of the most commonly used organization-based project selection indices. The first category includes quantitative indices (see Figure 1-1) that are generally based on financial characteristics, such as return on investment and net present value, cash flow, internal rate of return, cost-benefit analysis, and payback period. The second category includes qualitative indices (see Figure 1-2) that are intended to measure subjective issues, such as opera-

---

Figure 1-1
Quantitative Organizational Indices

Financial

- Total expected value of the portfolio
- Discounted cash flow of income from the deliverable
- Internal rate of return
- Net present value of earnings resulting from the project
- Expected commercialization value of the deliverable
- Time to break-even
- Total cost as a percentage of total available funds

Figure 1-2
Qualitative Organizational Indices

Strategic

- Probability of success of the deliverable
- Validity of the project vision
- Utility of the project deliverable
- Strategic importance
- Attractiveness of the deliverable
- Impact of the deliverable on the enterprise
- Benefits of the deliverable to the enterprise
- Duration of the project as compared to the urgency of the need for the deliverable

tional necessity, competitive necessity, product line extension, market constraints, desirability, recognition, and success.

Figure 1-3 depicts a generic selection model composed of four indices. The simple summation or weighted summation of the results of the indices will be used to compute the project's rating. Figure 1-4 shows a sample of a customized model. The possible total points for a project are 100; therefore, prospective projects can be compared on the basis of the total score. In this model, the importance of the indices, as signified by the points assigned to each, have been customized for a particular organization.

The relative importance of these indices is reflected by how many maximum possible points are assigned to each. For ex-

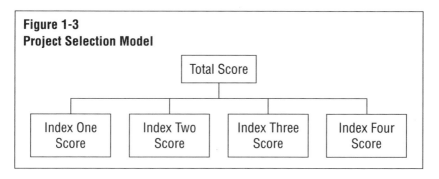

Figure 1-3
Project Selection Model

Total Score

Index One Score | Index Two Score | Index Three Score | Index Four Score

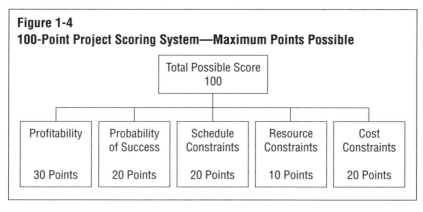

Figure 1-4
100-Point Project Scoring System—Maximum Points Possible

Total Possible Score
100

Profitability — 30 Points | Probability of Success — 20 Points | Schedule Constraints — 20 Points | Resource Constraints — 10 Points | Cost Constraints — 20 Points

ample, a hypothetical project might earn a total score of 60 points received on individual indices that were identified and ranked specifically for that organization (see Figure 1-5). The score of an individual project is not as important as the relative scores of several projects that were ranked using the same model and the same rating process.

When conducting project comparisons among a large pool of projects, normalizing the base of reference for cost and duration is useful and logical. One of the more convenient techniques is to use the direct cost as the base of reference for the prospective internal or external projects. Compartmentalizing the direct cost of the project from other elements has the advantage of developing a project estimate strictly from the standpoint of the level of effort. Other elements such as indirect costs, overhead, and return on investment are important values, but, because they tend to be somewhat variable with organizational entity and with time, they might add unnecessary inaccuracy to the project selection process. Normalization should then extend to equalizing the cost effects of the location of the project.

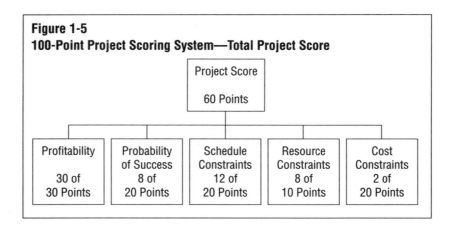

Figure 1-5
100-Point Project Scoring System—Total Project Score

The sophistication and accuracy of the initial project plans depend, to a great extent, on the amount of historical data collected in, or available to, the organization. The initial estimates of project cost and duration are used as part of the project selection process. Once the project is selected, the planning data are continually enhanced as more information about the project becomes available.

Estimating is a very inexact science during the early periods of the project life. Ironically, the very early estimates of a project become critical in determining whether the project reaches the next stage. Naturally, a detailed and focused set of project objectives enhances the accuracy of any given estimate and the probability of a project being selected.

Organizational strategic direction and deliverable expectations also play important roles in selecting a project. A formalized project selection procedure will include a prioritization model consisting of several quantified indices that reflect the project attributes as well as organizational priorities.

2 Work Breakdown Structure

The work breakdown structure (WBS) provides a framework for all project elements, for specific tasks within the project, and ultimately for better schedules and better estimates. A WBS will facilitate the process of integrating project plans for time, resources, and scope. A good WBS encourages a systematic planning process, reduces the possibility of omitting key project elements, and simplifies the project by dividing it into manageable units. If the WBS is used as the common skeleton for the schedule and for the estimate, it will facilitate communication among the project team members implementing the project.

The WBS is an exceptionally useful tool for project planning and monitoring, particularly if it is a deliverable-oriented structure. The information for a WBS is drawn primarily from the project objectives statement, historical files containing information on past projects, previous project performance reports, or any other files containing the original and final objectives of previous projects.

Rather than develop a WBS for each project, sometimes it is more convenient to develop a general WBS for a family of projects and then select and modify only selected segments for

This chapter is an adaptation of a paper by Parviz F. Rad, "Advocating a Deliverable-Oriented Work Breakdown Structure," that was originally published by AACE International in *Cost Engineering*, Volume 41, Issue 12, December 1999. Reprinted with the permission of AACE International, 209 Prairie Ave., Suite 100, Morgantown, WV 25601, USA. Phone 800-858-COST/304-296-8444. Fax: 304-291-5728. Internet: http://www.aacei.org. E-mail: info@aacei.org. Copyright © by AACE International; all rights reserved.

each project. This practice is appropriate in organizations that conduct projects that are somewhat similar but not necessarily identical.

The process of estimating the cost and duration of the project will also require a detailed and sophisticated resource breakdown structure (RBS). While the WBS is a methodical categorization of the deliverable's components, the RBS is a logical and useful classification of the resources necessary to accomplish the project objectives with respect to those deliverables. Rather than developing a new RBS for each project, developing an RBS for a large family of projects may be more efficient. As each new project is planned, only those portions of this common RBS that apply to the project at hand will be selected and used.

A project RBS is different from all other human resource or budgeting classification methods in that it will reflect applicability to project management as compared to cost accounting or to personnel evaluations. An RBS is essentially a catalog of all the resources that will be available to the project.

Another readily available structure that is indirectly useful to project planning is the organizational breakdown structure (OBS). Because companies frequently go through massive organizational changes, care must be taken to use the most current data, keeping them current with frequent updates as changes continue to occur to the reporting lines of the organization. For the purposes of the project management system, the normal organizational chart must be augmented by those unwritten responsibilities and by those dotted-line relationships that affect the project's execution. The OBS will be exceptionally useful in identifying project stakeholders, organizational objectives, and resource constraints.

A WBS is—or should be—a uniform, consistent, and logical method for dividing the project into small, manageable components for purposes of planning, estimating, and monitoring. The WBS is also a facilitative tool for communication between the team and the stakeholders, and among the team members. A WBS will provide a roadmap for planning, monitoring, and managing all facets of the project, such as:

- Definition of work

- Cost estimates

- Budgeting

- Time estimates

- Scheduling

- Resource allocation

- Expenditures

- Changes to the project plan

- Productivity

- Performance.

As the project is conceived, defined, and fully developed, not only can summaries for the WBS be created for one project, but departmental and divisional summaries also can be made for each WBS item. These summaries, which use the relationship between the WBS, RBS, and the resource expenditure profile, can be quite useful for resource forecasting, personnel projections, priority definitions among projects, assessing the performance of departments and divisions, and general management purposes.

WBS DEVELOPMENT STEPS

Simply stated, WBS development can be viewed as the process of grouping all project elements into several major categories, normally referred to as Level One; each one of these categories will itself contain several subcategories, normally referred to as Level Two. Alternately, and more accurately, developing a WBS involves dividing the project into many parts that, when combined, constitute the project deliverable.

As a rule of thumb, the project is divided into several (three to nine) elements (see Figure 2-1). Then, each of the Level One elements will be divided into three to nine Level Two elements, each of the Level Two elements will be divided into three to nine Level Three elements, and so on. The ultimate goal is to formulate a detailed WBS that highlights a logical organization of products, parts, and modules.

This process of dividing the deliverable items continues until the project has been divided into manageable, discrete, and identifiable items requiring simple tasks to complete. A rule of thumb is to keep dividing the project until the elements cannot realistically be divided anymore. This point may vary from organization to organization and may even vary among project managers within the same organization.

The contents of each level of detail are not only organization-specific, but they also are specific to the nature of the deliverables involved in each project. Similarly, the degree of detail at the lowest level of each branch must be in line with the size of the project and in conformance with the organization's operational philosophies.

Figure 2-1
Work Breakdown Structure

- Divide the work into 3–9 categories
- Divide each category into 3–9 packages
- Divide each package into 3–9 modules
- Divide . . . .
- Divide . . . .
- Divide . . . .

Ideally, there should be some uniformity and consistency in the WBS. To achieve this uniformity, all children of the same parent must be developed based on the same division basis.

Reasonable consistency should be maintained in the degree of detail at the lowest level elements. For example, if one branch describes the transmission of a car and the other branch describes the engine of the same car, the lowest levels should go either to subcomponents such as valves and sensors, or to more detail down to the metal screws. Not all branches need to go to the same level, but the significance of all of the lowest-level items in the overall project should be similar. Therefore, depending on the nature of the project, some branches may go to Level Two, some to Level Three, and some to Level Five.

Several WBS examples are included at the end of this chapter.

THE DIVISION BASES

The transition from each level of WBS to the next level may be based on any one of the following (see Figure 2-2):

- Deliverables

- Schedules

- Resources.

Figure 2-2
Work Breakdown Structure

1. Deliverable-oriented	2. Schedule-oriented	3. Resource-oriented
• Product	• Task or activity	• Disciplines
• Functional system	• Sequential (phases)	• Administrative units
• Physical area		• Financial accounts
• Proof of capability		

In the deliverable-oriented mode, the product basis refers to those cases in which the project is divided into individual distinct components that ultimately comprise the project, such as hardware, software, physical structure, concrete foundation, or steel roof. The functional basis refers to the functional systems that provide a particular facet of the infrastructure for the project deliverable. Functional systems usually are interwoven into the product. Examples of functional systems include the electrical system, mechanical system, or skeleton of a building. In software and system development projects, these could be the verification module, data transfer module, backup module, and virus protection module. The physical-area basis highlights the geographical or physical locations of the deliverable (e.g., south side, north side, top floor, entrance). The most useful, and admittedly the most difficult, procedure for developing a WBS is to use the deliverable as the basis of breakdown of the project.

There is some overlap in definition and usage among the items of a subgroup of these nine bases, i.e., among product, functional system, and physical location. It is possible that someone would divide the project on the basis of product, and, depending on the nature of the project, someone else might view the division as having been on the basis of physical location.

For example, if the deliverables of a project included an industrial plan, one could divide the deliverables by functions, such as receiving, fabricating, polishing, packaging, and shipping. These operational functions use pieces of equipment that are distinct products, and operational design requires that each function be located in a specific area of the floor. Therefore, the division basis can be regarded as physical location basis also. Regardless of which of these subcategories is used, the deliverable basis of WBS development is far superior to the other bases, partly because it is customer-focused and partly because it has profound facilitation features during the project's execution stages.

In the schedule-oriented mode, task or activity basis refers to things that project team members do toward accomplishing the goals of the project, such as excavating, pouring, forming, polishing, programming, and testing. Sequential basis reflects the order in which activities are performed, such as Phase I, Phase II, and Phase III. The sequence often is dictated by administrative constraints and is somewhat arbitrary.

Using these two bases is akin to importing the project schedule into the WBS. Ideally, the WBS should be used to develop the schedule, and not the other way around. There is no question that the lowest level of a fully developed WBS will comprise activities. However, it would be more useful if one of the deliverable-oriented bases were used for the majority of the upper portion of the structure.

Similarly, the resource-oriented basis is an infusion of the organizational structure into the WBS and will highlight the administrative or organizational division lines. Examples of discipline, or administrative-unit, basis elements are work done by employees of division A, division B, or the contract office.

The budget account basis is an infusion of the resource availability profile into the WBS and will follow the organization's financial structure, such as activities paid by federal funds, state funds, charge account A, or fiscal account B. Here again, the WBS should be used to develop the cost accounts, costs estimates, and resource assignments, and not the other way around. The distinction is that funding procedures should not influence the nature of the project, just how the costs are disbursed.

COMPARISON OF THE DIFFERENT BASES

The most common and easiest method of developing the WBS is to use the task, activity, or phase as the basis of breakdown from one level to another. The vast majority of the elements in the vast majority of WBS fit this pattern. By and large, the project professionals that come from a scheduling background tend to use this basis as the breakdown basis. Notwithstanding, the deliverable-oriented bases, using any of the deliverable subcategories shown in Figure 2-1, are preferable.

One stated advantage for the schedule-oriented elements is that the resulting WBS can be used for many projects. Although this feature can be an advantage because the WBS is generic, the same feature also can be a disadvantage because it does not address the definitive features of the project in a clear and highlighted fashion.

Another feature of a schedule-oriented WBS, which sometimes has been perceived as an advantage, is that the WBS is applicable when the project is not fully defined. Unfortunately, this advantage also becomes a disadvantage when the project is fully specified, yet the estimating and scheduling of the project are still dependent on bundled categories for items such as design and testing.

Because ultimately projects are carried out when people do things such as develop, draw, print, fix, and fabricate, the elements at the lowest level always will be activity-based. However, using the deliverable methodology, the basis of division would change from schedule-oriented to deliverable-oriented as low in the WBS as possible. Alternately, different activities can be signaled by assigning resources that have appropriate titles or functions. For example, a lowest-level element can be tagged to design engineers, software programmers, and test engineers. Thus, without listing an activity-based WBS element, we have identified the activities involved with this element, namely, designing, programming, and testing.

The second most common basis for developing a WBS is the administrative basis. Those project professionals who come from a financial or administrative background tend to use disciplines, administrative units, or budget accounts as the basis of WBS breakdown. Although such bases would make tracking funds very simple and straightforward, they may not significantly help the project management objectives. The bases included in the resource-oriented group should be used as little as possible because they do not refer to the deliverable but rather to the means by which the work intended to produce the deliverable is administered and paid for.

Even if one chooses a schedule-based WBS, it is very important to make sure that the elements on the first several levels of the WBS, certainly those on Level One, are deliverable-oriented and not schedule-oriented or resource-oriented. That is not to say that activities and costs are not important. On the contrary, development, monitoring, analysis, and control of project schedule and project financing will be far more meaningful if a deliverable-oriented WBS that includes activities, or activity-referenced resources, at the lowest levels is used.

For example, if the testing tasks are late, it would be possible to determine that the complexity of testing Item BB has delayed the overall testing results. Similarly, if the design costs are significantly below budget, it would be possible to determine that an unexpected reduction in component design costs for item CC has caused this unexpected (and pleasant) reduction.

With minimal effort, deliverable-oriented elements can easily be developed for the top levels of the WBS for most projects. Beyond that, product-oriented projects can easily include deliverable-oriented WBS elements for most of the project, sometimes with the exception of the first or second levels. This methodical approach may initially require some extra effort for those project managers who have used schedule-oriented WBS in the past. Once using this methodology becomes second nature, deliverable-oriented WBS can be developed with ease. Process-oriented projects tend to have schedule-oriented elements for most of their WBS, certainly at the lower portion.

A deliverable-oriented WBS is most useful in projects in which it is more important to know the scope, cost, and duration of each delivered module rather than the activities that produced that module or group of modules. By contrast, a schedule-oriented WBS is more appropriate for cost-plus projects, for internal projects that have no work packages to contract, and for projects where the activities or the-step-by-step process is of utmost importance. Additionally, a deliverable-oriented WBS would facilitate and encourage the feed-forward of information within the project. (Feed-forward is a process by which the estimate of an element is refined by the performance of similar elements that were implemented earlier in the same project.)

PROCESS-ORIENTED PROJECTS

The point in the WBS at which the basis of division will change from deliverable-oriented to schedule-oriented depends on the nature of the project. If the project involves delivering a physical entity, most of the divisions and elements other than the lowest level can easily be described with deliverables. If the project is process-oriented, most of the elements will be activities.

A project is product-oriented if, at its end, a unique final product is delivered to the client, such as a car, an airplane, a building, an organizational structure, or a set of design documents. By contrast, a process-oriented project is somewhat repetitive, such as running a lumber mill, a refinery, or a contamination cleanup project. In these cases, the project resembles a checklist of objectives that must be estimated and scheduled. Even in these projects, someone fully conversant with the deliverable WBS can develop deliverable elements.

It is difficult—although not impossible, and certainly advisable—to develop deliverable-oriented elements for the top levels of the WBS for most of the process-oriented projects. The difficulty in developing a deliverable-oriented WBS is minor for projects that involve physical results, and the difficulty can be significant for process-oriented projects.

Sometimes, the distinction between a product-oriented project and a process-oriented project is determined by testing whether or not the project activities have become somewhat standardized in developing replicas of the deliverable of the first project. To illustrate, designing and building the first supersonic jumbo jet is a product-oriented project. However, manufacturing each of the next 245 planes is a process-oriented project.

In some projects, in which the physical deliverables are minimal or not commonly recognized as deliverables, the majority of elements are schedule-oriented. Examples of these projects are cleaning up a contaminated site, demolishing a building, excavating the cavity for a building foundation, or removing a software virus from a computer program. With some effort, a deliverable-based WBS can be crafted even for these projects. For example, the deliverable items can be reports of test results for thickness, contaminants, texture, or color. Likewise, the deliverables can be reports of test results for error rate, customer satisfaction, processing speed, and transmission speed.

Additional examples of product-oriented projects are:

- A new bank

- A new laboratory

- A new manufacturing plant

- A new software package

- A software upgrade

- A unique facility design.

By contrast, examples of process-oriented projects are:

- Conducting the annual closeout at a bank

- Converting chemicals into plastics

- Converting crude oil to gasoline

- Performing annual turnaround or maintenance for factories and plants

- Manufacturing a batch of chemicals

- Monitoring productivity at Site G

- Issuing monthly payroll checks.

ORGANIZATIONAL PRIORITIES

Sometimes there is a tendency to add items to the WBS that do not represent deliverables but that are activities that are part of the organizational priorities and imperatives. The intent of including such items in the first level of WBS is to signal conformance with the organizational imperatives or to maintain organizational harmony. Examples of items that often find their way to the first level of WBS are:

- User support

- Purchasing

- Integration

- Systems engineering

- Value engineering

- Contract process

- Project monitoring

- Project management

- Budget approval

- Project closeout

- Reporting

- Design process.

The rationale for not including these items at Level One is two-fold. First, it would distort the deliverable basis of division at Level One; Level One would be fully deliverable without this activity element, and a hybrid of sorts with that activity. Second, and more important, placing such activities at Level One would detract from the accuracy of the plans and would thus destroy the sharp focus necessary for monitoring the schedule and cost. With some amount of care, these items either can be rolled into the overhead cost of the project or they can be tagged to individual lowest-level elements, or activities, as resources—that is, of course, if there is no overriding organizational need to highlight these elements.

An example of such a WBS modification was observed during the WBS development for a project with the objective to deliver a computer system to a customer. This project involved providing software and hardware to the client at the end of the project. The elements of this WBS were deliverable-oriented through Level Four (see Figure 2-3). The Level One WBS items were:

- Hardware

- Software

- System documents.

After the WBS was developed, the divisional manager instructed the project manager to add user support as a Level-One element. The reason was that, at the time, the organization was making a transition toward more user-friendly systems development. Inserting user support as a first-level WBS item was intended to recognize and highlight this priority. Therefore, the Level One elements of this systems development WBS became (see Figure 2-4):

Figure 2-3
System Development

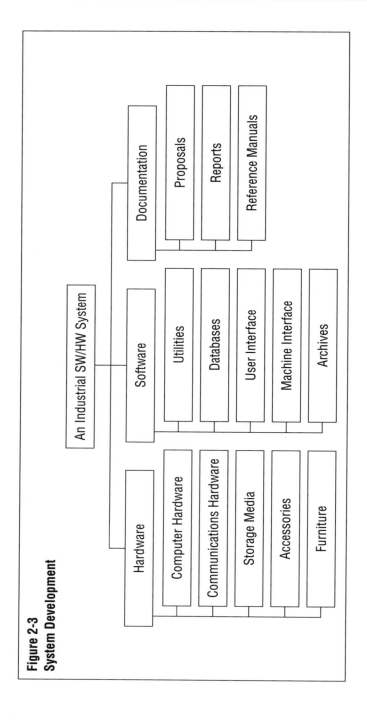

Figure 2-4
WBS Organizational Priorities Added

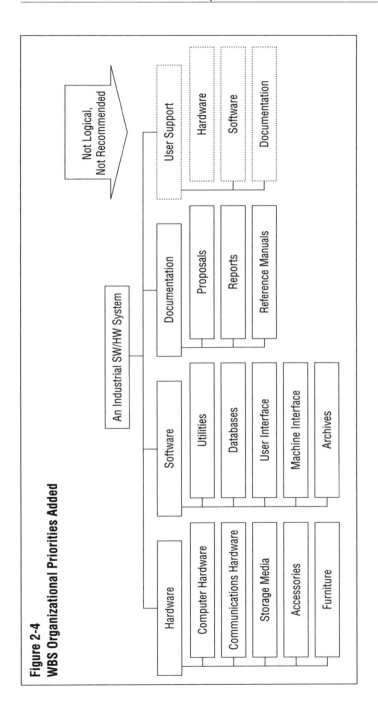

- Hardware

- Software

- System documents

- User support.

The disadvantage of listing these activities as Level One items is that they become freestanding activities that seemingly are not associated with any specific product. The amorphous nature of the task also makes it difficult, if not impossible, to monitor and control the resource expenditures with any reasonable accuracy. Certainly, these activities are needed to deliver the products that are listed on Level Three or Level Four of the WBS, and they need to be listed as such.

Moreover, even if these activities are listed at lower levels, they can be summarized with equal ease across WBS structures and across resource structures. The only difference is that, using a fully deliverable structure, they are not highlighted at Level One of the WBS. Admittedly, listing these activities at Level One might afford very high visibility to the upper management for these activities, primarily because upper management usually gets to see only the first two levels of the WBS. Again, such augmentation of the WBS distorts the logical structure of the WBS and therefore is not recommended.

SEMANTICS

Using vague words or words with multiple meaning in WBS titles can cause confusion and misunderstandings in interpreting and planning the WBS items. For example, if a WBS item is labeled "procurement," it could refer to the people who buy things, the department that employs them, or the process of buying things. Similarly, if a WBS item is labeled "mechanical," it could refer to the mechanical engineering design process, the mechanical portion of the deliverables, the mechanical engineers, or the department that employs them. If a WBS item is labeled "system," it could refer to the system that is delivered to the client, the software portion of the system, the people who write the software, the department that employs them, or the process of writing software (see Figure 2-5).

Admittedly, most of the time the likelihood of confusion and misunderstanding is minimized if these words are interpreted within the appropriate context. However, the project planner must make every effort to eliminate all potential causes of confusion from the project plans.

As an illustration, consider a project that is described by the following WBS components: procurement, systems, civil, mechanical, and legal. These elements could be interpreted as uniformly referring to disciplines, administrative units, activities, or a combination of the above (see Figure 2-6). If there is a possibility of ambiguity in naming the WBS elements, qualifiers such as "mechanical engineering department," "civil engineers," "Procurement Phase II," "software module," "mechanical drawings," or "contract documents" should eliminate any confusion.

CHANGING THE PARADIGM

A WBS sometimes can be changed from schedule-oriented to deliverable-oriented by modifying and changing the wording of some elements. However, the transition from a schedule-

Figure 2-5
WBS Complications

- System (could refer to):
  - System that is delivered to client
  - Software portion of the system
  - People who write the software
  - Department that employs them
  - Process of writing software

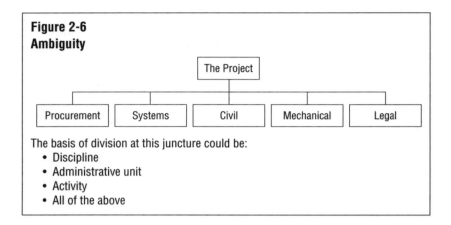

Figure 2-6
Ambiguity

The basis of division at this juncture could be:
• Discipline
• Administrative unit
• Activity
• All of the above

oriented WBS to a deliverable-oriented WBS is not simply effected by using non-action words; rather, it involves looking at the project from the standpoint of the client. Thus, the WBS would include the elements that the client is interested in receiving and those that the client will pay for.

One way of highlighting the deliverable-oriented basis is to emphasize that the deliverable-based approach is client-centric and not project team-centric. As the WBS is developed, therefore, the project management professionals should be careful not to infuse details of how the work will be delivered into the description of the deliverable itself.

Once a deliverable-oriented WBS is established, if the client changes the scope and schedule constraint of various project modules, it is very easy to determine and justify the impact of such changes on the cost and schedule of the project. The reason is that planning a project with a deliverable-oriented WBS is conducted by planning specific items that make up the project, and not by planning a bundle of generic activities involved in delivering those items. Equally important, when the time comes to make those inevitable changes to the project plan, they can be made more accurately and logically with the use of deliverable items because the changes will be reflected only in those items that are affected.

The transition from a schedule-oriented WBS to a deliverable-oriented WBS may be difficult for those who have developed schedule-oriented WBS for a significant amount of time. The transition should be guided by a change in mindset from team-centric to client-centric. The focus should be on project objectives and specifications rather than on the activities of the team.

In cases in which the project objectives are not fully developed at the time the WBS is crafted, only the first two or three levels of the WBS can be developed. Later, as more project information becomes available, the WBS can be expanded and refined. Actually, this is a major advantage because it highlights the organic nature of the project plans.

Conceptually, the process of developing a deliverable-oriented WBS is relatively simple. One would divide the project into components that, when combined, would produce the final project deliverable. Ideally, one should avoid converting elements to activities and tasks until the last one or two levels of the WBS. The emphasis should be on describing the components that produce the project, the modules that produce the component, the units that produce the module, etc.

Additionally, one should avoid listing (as part of the WBS structure) the personnel responsible for delivery of reports, evaluations, or products. Such resource assignments can be done easily and systematically once the WBS and RBS are established, preferably independently of each other. An effective way to achieve this is to develop an RBS before starting to divide the project objectives, so that the project planner will not be distracted by resource issues during WBS development.

The following is the first level of a WBS that was developed using the traditional schedule-oriented mindset (see Figure 2-7):

Level One

- Conceptual design

Figure 2-7
Schedule-Oriented WBS

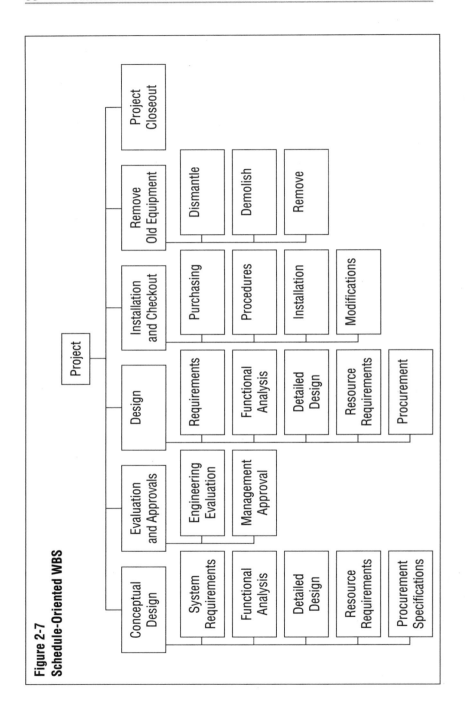

- Evaluation and approvals

- Design

- Installation and checkout

- Removal of old equipment

- Project closeout.

Because a schedule-oriented WBS tends to be entirely activity-based, it is very difficult if not impossible to discern what the objective of the project is and what its deliverables are. Although not clearly identified in the WBS, the objective of this project is to deliver the following:

- Two new emission stacks

- New emissions monitoring system

- Emergency power building.

Accordingly, a deliverable-based WBS could be constructed along the lines of the following (see Figure 2-8):

Level One

- Design documents

- Building structure

- Emergency generator system

- Stack monitors

- Stacks.

This WBS clearly describes what the client should expect from the project manager or the contractor when the project is finished. Accordingly, tracking the project's progress would be

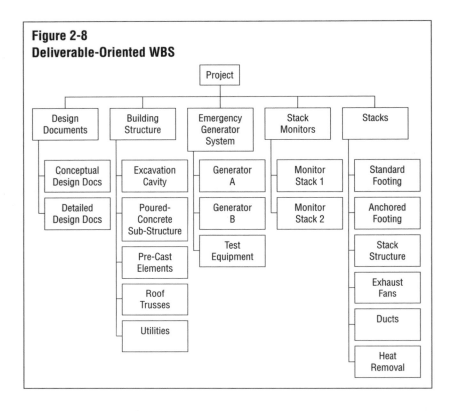

Figure 2-8
Deliverable-Oriented WBS

relatively simple by noting the progress of the delivery of the project's components.

This example illustrates that with the deliverable-oriented WBS, one can easily and clearly plan the components of the project as a prelude to an informed process for monitoring the progress of the project's components. One gets a clear idea of the project objectives and what is involved in achieving them. A deliverable-oriented WBS is easier to schedule, estimate, and monitor. Depending on the size of the project and the traditions of this particular environment, either the next level of activities would be schedule-oriented elements, or the element would be tagged to use activity-specific resources.

EXAMPLE

The following example illustrates use of the deliverable-oriented and the schedule-oriented bases for a fictional industrial complex (see Figure 2-9). The division of elements at different junctures has been performed using different bases.

- Power House

    - Steam generation system

    - Electrical generation system

    - Electrical transmission system

- Factory

    - Receiving equipment

    - Processing equipment

    - Packaging equipment

    - Shipping equipment

- Office

    - First floor

    - Second floor

    - Penthouse

- Grounds

    - Phase One: bushes and trees

    - Phase Two: seeding for lawn

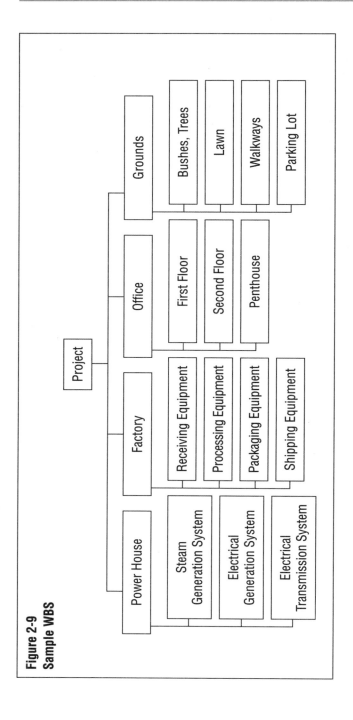

Figure 2-9
Sample WBS

- Phase Three: walkways

- Phase Four: parking lot.

In this example, the breakdown basis for Level One is physical location; for the powerhouse, functional system; for the factory, product, physical location, or functional system; for the office, physical location; and for the grounds, sequential. If this project were to be implemented, a new all-deliverable WBS could and should be developed.

The WBS is the most important element of the planning process. A carefully organized WBS will set the foundation for planning the details of a logical and integrated project data baseline that will benefit all other aspects of the project, particularly estimating and scheduling.

Three separate and distinct methods can be used to break the project into smaller and manageable pieces: deliverable, schedule, and resource. The deliverable basis is the most useful and preferred of the three. A well-defined, deliverable-oriented WBS will facilitate unambiguous planning, accurate reporting, and regular updating. Deliverable-oriented elements can be developed for the top levels of the WBS for most projects with relative ease. Although developing deliverable-oriented WBS elements at lower levels may initially require some extra effort for those who have used schedule-oriented WBS in the past, deliverable-oriented WBS can be developed for most projects with nominal effort once this process becomes second nature for project managers.

Work Breakdown Structure Examples

Home Building Project

Hardware Design Project

Health Services Project

Bank Data Conversion Software Project

Wireless Communications Project

Branch Network Restructuring Project

Industrial Construction Project

Home Building Project

Deliverable Work Breakdown Structure

0.0. Residential House
- 1.0 Project Documents
  - 1.1 Contractual Documents
    - 1.1.1 Proposal
    - 1.1.2 Quotation
    - 1.1.3 Contract
  - 1.2 Drawings
    - 1.2.1 Architectural Drawings
    - 1.2.2 Civil Drawings
    - 1.2.3 Electrical System Drawings
    - 1.2.4 Mechanical System Drawings
  - 1.3 Permits
    - 1.3.1 Zoning
    - 1.3.2 Labor
    - 1.3.3 Building Inspection
  - 1.4 Project Controls
    - 1.4.1 Schedule
    - 1.4.2 Cost Estimate
    - 1.4.3 Risk Management Plan
- 2.0 Project Supplies
  - 2.1 Raw Materials
    - 2.1.1 Architectural Finish Materials
    - 2.1.2 Civil Structure Materials
    - 2.1.3 Electrical Systems Materials
    - 2.1.4 Mechanical Systems Materials
  - 2.2 Manufactured Components (machines, parts, etc.)
    - 2.2.1 Architectural Equipment
    - 2.2.2 Civil Structure Equipment
    - 2.2.3 Electrical Systems Equipment
    - 2.2.4 Mechanical Systems Equipment
  - 2.3 Specialty Equipment
- 3.0 Project Edifice (the "house")
  - 3.1 Civil Structure
    - 3.1.1 Land
    - 3.1.2 Foundation
    - 3.1.3 Superstrucutre
      - 3.1.3.1 Floors
      - 3.1.3.2 Framing
      - 3.1.3.3 Roof

3.2 Mechanical Systems
    3.2.1 Potable Water System
    3.2.2 Sewage System
    3.2.3 HVAC Systems
        3.2.4.1 Heating
        3.2.4.2 Air Conditioning
        3.2.4.3 Ventilation
3.3 Electrical Systems
    3.3.1 Electricity Distribution System
    3.3.2 Phone/LAN Lines
    3.3.3 Fire Detection System
    3.3.4 Home Security System
3.4 Architectural Finishes
    3.4.1 Basement
    3.4.2 First Floor
    3.4.3 Second Floor
    3.4.4 Exterior

Hardware Design Project

Work Breakdown Structure

0.0 ABC123 Integrated circuit database
1.0 Circuit design schematics
    1.1 Base-level Schematics
        1.1.1 Multiplexer 1
        1.1.2 Multiplexed
        1.1.3 Rotational frequency detector
        1.1.4 Variable controlled oscillator
        1.1.5 Digital/analog converter
        1.1.6 Counter I
        1.1.7 Counter 2
    1.2 Block-level Schematics
        1.2.1 Equalizer
        1.2.2 CDRPLL
        1.2.3 Transmitter PLL
        1.2.4 LVDS driver
        1.2.5 Decoder
        1.2.6 Encoder
        1.2.7 Cable driver
    1.3 Top-level schematic
2.0 Mask Design cells
    2.1 Base-level cells
        2.1.1 Multiplexer 1
        2.1.2 Multiplexed
        2.1.3 Rotational frequency detector
        2.1.4 Variable controlled oscillator
        2.1.5 Digital/analog converter
        2.1.6 Counter I
        2.1.7 Counter 2
    2.2 Block-level cells
        2.2.1 Equalizer
        2.2.2 CDR PLL
        2.2.3 Transmitter PLL
        2.2.4 LVDS driver
        2.2.5 Decoder
        2.2.6 Encoder
        2.2.7 Cable driver
    2.3 Top-level cell
3.0 Documentation

3.1 NPPRS Deliverables
    3.1.1 Product requirement specification
    3.1.2 Intellectual property plan
    3.1.3 CAD and design library development plan
    3.1.4 Project risk analysis
    3.1.5 Design FMEA
    3.1.6 Business case
    3.1.7 Buildsheet
    3.1.8 DRC/LVS report
    3.1.9 Patent applications
    3.1.10 Final design review
3.2 Supplemental design documents
    3.2.1 Intermediate circuit design reviews
        3.2.1.1 Equalizer
        3.2.1.2 CDRPLL
        3.2.1.3 Transmitter PLL
        3.2.1.4 Multiplexer
        3.2.1.5 Multiplexed
        3.2.1.6 LVDS driver
        3.2.1.7 Decoder
        3.2.1.8 Encoder.
        3.2.1.9 Cable driver
    3.2.2 Mask design reviews
        3.2.2.1 CDRPLL
        3.2.2.2 Transmitter PLL
        3.2.2.3 Cable driver
        3.2.2.4 Equalizer
        3.2.2.5 Top-level floorplan review
3.3 Miscellaneous documents
    3.3.1 Weekly project review
    3.3.2 HSPICE model
    3.3.3 DFT analysis

Terms:

Buildsheet   A document that graphically represents the package assembly requirements for a specific integrated circuit. Package DRCs are performed while generating this document.

CDR PLL   Clock/Data Recovery Phase-Locked Loop

DFT   Design for testability. A DFT analysis is performed on the circuit to decide if additional circuitry is needed to enable various aspects of the circuit's functionality to be verified once the physical IC is being produced.

DRC/LVS   Design Rules Check/Layout vs. Schematic.

FMEA   Failure Mode Effects Analysis

HSPICE   Software used to generate models of a circuit that customers can use to integrate into their system design model to test functionality.

LVDS   Low Voltage Differential Signal

NIBU   Network Interface Business Unit, a business unit within the Wired Communications Division of National Semiconductor.

NPPRS   Network Interface Business Unit's New Product Phase Review System is the structured stage-gate process utilized to develop new products, in which the deliverables at each phase are clearly defined.

Weekly Project Review   Due to the duration of the design portion of this project, weekly project reviews are generated for middle and upper management and the team. The reviews encompass all nine areas of project management as shown in the RBS.

Health Services Project

Work Breakdown Schedule

Outpatient Occupational Therapy Center—Work Breakdown Structure

1   Facility
   1.1   Location
      1.1.1   Site
      1.1.2   Leasing contract
      1.1.3   Possession
   1.2   Interior
      1.2.1   Office
         1.2.1.1   Information desk
         1.2.1.2   Individual office space for employees
         1.2.1.3   Records library
      1.2.2   Occupational Therapy Department
         1.2.2.1   Diagnostic and Evaluation rooms
            1.2.2.1.1   Area for physical evaluation
            1.2.2.1.2   Area for neurological evaluation
            1.2.2.1.3   Area for cognitive evaluation
            1.2.2.1.4   Area for pediatric evaluation
         1.2.2.2   Therapeutic rooms
            1.2.2.2.1   Area for physical therapy
            1.2.2.2.2   Area for neurological therapy
            1.2.2.2.3   Area for cognitive therapy
            1.2.2.2.4   Area for pediatric therapy
         1.2.2.3   Rehabilitative rooms
            1.2.2.3.1   Area for physical rehabilitation
            1.2.2.3.2   Area for neurological rehabilitation
            1.2.2.3.3   Area for cognitive rehabilitation
            1.2.2.3.4   Area for pediatric rehabilitation
      1.2.3   Miscellaneous
         1.2.3.1   Waiting area
         1.2.3.2   Kitchen
         1.2.3.3   Restrooms
   1.3   Exterior
      1.3.1   Security system
      1.3.2   Access to physically handicapped
      1.3.3   Billboard of facility name
2   Personnel
   2.1   Occupational therapy professionals
      2.1.1   Registered occupational therapist
      2.1.2   Certified occupational therapy assistant
      2.1.3   Occupational therapy counselor

2.1.4 Registered nurse

2.1.5 Medical assistant

2.2 Support Staff

2.2.1 Social worker

2.2.2 Home health aide

2.2.3 Nursing aide

2.2.4 Equipment maintenance specialist

2.2.5 Maid and housekeeper

2.2.6 Security guard

2.2.7 Financial advisor for patients

2.3 Administrative Staff

2.3.1 Receptionist and information desk clerk

2.3.2 Administrative assistant

2.3.3 Accountant

3 Licenses

3.1 Business

3.2 Registered occupational therapist

3.3 Certified occupational therapy assistant

3.4 Registered nurse

3.5 Software

4 Insurance

4.1 Business

4.2 Registered occupational therapist

4.3 Certified occupational therapy assistant

4.4 Registered nurse

4.5 Warranties and insurance on equipment

5 Operations

5.1 Maintenance

5.1.1 Inventories

5.1.2 Equipment

5.1.3 Housekeeping

5.2 Human Resources

5.2.1 Payroll services

5.2.2 Employee benefits

5.2.3 Continued recruiting

5.3 Client Services

5.3.1 Administrative

5.3.1.1 Appointments

5.3.1.2 Paperwork

5.3.1.3 Insurance claims

5.3.2 Therapeutic

5.3.2.1 Diagnosis and evaluation

5.3.2.2 Therapeutic or rehabilitative treatment

5.3.2.3 Follow-up

Bank Data Conversion Software Project

XYZ Corporation Global Services
Conversion Services Contracted Core
Banking Data Conversion

Objectives

This project provides data from an acquired bank converted to a format that allows merging of the data into the client's applications. The project includes needs assessment, application and process design, implementation, and creation of the converted files and reports for client testing.

Work Breakdown Structure
0. Banking Data Conversion
   1.0 Functioning Environment
      1.1 Project Execution Environment
      1.2 Host System Environment
      1.3 Remote Network Environment
      1.4 Workstation Environment
   2.0 Needs Analysis Documentation
      2.1 Source System Analysis Report
      2.2 Source Data Dictionary
      2.3 Source Data Analysis Report
         2.3.1 Customer Information File Analysis Report
         2.3.2 Name & Address Scrubbing Analysis Report
         2.3.3 Account File Analysis Report
         2.3.4 Account History File Analysis Report
         2.3.5 Pre-Authorized Transaction File Analysis Report
         2.3.6 Product Definition Table Analysis Report
      2.4 Target System Analysis Report
   3.0 Design Documentation
      3.1 Overall Solution Approach Document
      3.2 Product Definition Report
      3.3 Target Record Layout Definition
      3.4 Detailed Schedule of Mapping Sessions
      3.5 Mapping Specifications
         3.5.1 Customer Information File Specs
         3.5.2 Account File Specs
         3.5.3 Account History File Specs
         3.5.4 Pre-Authorized Transaction File Specs
         3.5.5 Product Definition Table Specs
      3.6 Balancing Documentation
      3.7 Solution Approach Document

Wireless Communications Project

Upon completion of the relocation, a new RFT will be located in Las Vegas, all customer netgroups will be up and running in the new facility, and customer backhaul networks will be installed and functional. The Los Angeles facility will be returned to the landlord according to the conditions of the lease.

0.0 Relocation of Los Angeles Shared Hub Facility
   1.0 Equipment
      1.1 RFT Equipment
         1.1.1 New Indoor Equipment
         1.1.2 Old Indoor Equipment
         1.1.3 New Outdoor Equipment
         1.1.4 Old Outdoor Equipment
         1.1.5 New Cabling
         1.1.6 Old Cabling
      1.2 Baseband Equipment
         1.2.1 Spare NG A/B
         1.2.2 NG1/2
         1.2.3 NG3/4
         1.2.4 NG5/6
         1.2.5 NG7/8
         1.2.6 NG 9/10
      1.3 Backhaul Equipment and Lines
         1.3.1 Hub Routers
         1.3.2 Customer Routers
         1.3.3 T-Lines
   2.0 Facility
      2.1 Las Vegas
         2.1.1 Land
         2.1.2 Antenna Foundation
         2.1.3 Building Infrastructure
      2.2 Restoration of Los Angeles
         2.2.1 Restore-Land
         2.2.2 Restore-Foundation
         2.2.3 Restore-Building Infrastructure
   3.0 Documentation
      3.1 Project Controls
         3.1.1 Schedule
         3.1.2 Cost Estimate
         3.1.3 Risk Management Plan
      3.2 Drawings/Plans
         3.2.1 RFT Design
         3.2.2 Baseband Design
         3.2.3 Backhaul Design
         3.2.4 Facility Design

3.3 Permits
    3.3.1 Zoning
    3.3.2 Labor
    3.3.3 Environmental Approval
4.0 Personnel
    4.1 Staffing Plan
    4.2 Relocation Plan for existing personnel to Las Vegas
    4.3 Training

Branch Network Restructuring Project

Work Breakdown Structure

Deliverable Oriented

PROJECT'S OBJECTIVES STATEMENT

Design and implement a new salary, incentive, and responsibility structure for the branch network positions that recognizes and rewards employees for their role in the organization and for contributing to the bank's success.

Level 0	Level 1	Level 2	Level 3	Level 4	Deliverable Defined
0 Branch Network Restructuring Project					
	1.1 Branch Network Definition				Document that clearly defines how the branch network will assist the bank in meeting its objectives
		1.1.1 Bank Goals			Document that defines the overall bank goals
			1.1.1.1 Mission Statement		Document prepared by senior management identifying the general mission of the bank
			1.1.1.2 Strategic Plan		Document prepared by senior management identifying the 1-3-5-year strategy for the bank
		1.1.2 Strategic Alignment			Document identifying strategic alignment of teller and FSR position
			1.1.2.1 Teller Position		Document identifying teller's role in bank's strategy
			1.1.2.2 FSR Position		Document identifying FSR's role in bank's strategy
	1.2 Position Analysis				Document summarizing the current state of the branch network positions
		1.2.1 Teller Position Analysis			Document summarizing the current state of the teller position
			1.2.1.1 Incumbent Interviews		Document summarizing results of interviews with current tellers

1.2.1.2	Management Interviews	Document summarizing results of interviews regarding teller position with managers
1.2.1.3	Monitoring Reports	Document summarizing results of review of teller monitoring reports
1.2.1.4	Performance Reviews	Document summarizing results of analysis of completed teller reviews
1.2.1.5	Job Descriptions	Document summarizing results of analysis of current teller job description
1.2.1.6	Pay Scale	Document summarizing results of analysis of teller pay scale as related to job responsibilities and other like positions in the organization
	1.2.1.6.1 Responsibility Requirements	Document identifying teller position responsibilities as compared to other like positions
1.2.2	FSR Position Analysis	Document summarizing the current state of the FSR position
1.2.2.1	Incumbent Interviews	Document summarizing results of interviews with current FSRs
1.2.2.2	Management Interviews	Document summarizing results of interviews regarding FSR position with managers
1.2.2.3	Monitoring Reports	Document summarizing results of reviews of FSR monitoring reports
1.2.2.4	Performance Reviews	Document summarizing results of analysis of completed FSR reviews
1.2.2.5	Job Descriptions	Document summarizing results of analysis of current FSR job description
1.2.2.6	Pay Scale	Document summarizing results of analysis of FSR pay scale as related to job responsibilities and other like positions in the organization
1.2.2.7	Responsibility Requirements	Document identifying FSR position responsibilities as compared to other like positions
1.3 Solution Design		Document proposing solutions to branch network issues identified during analysis phase
1.3.1	Teller Solution Design	Document proposing solutions to teller issues identified during analysis phase
1.3.1.1	Hierarchy	Document proposing new hierarchical relationship of the teller position
1.3.1.2	Incentives	Document proposing new teller incentive plan
1.3.1.3	Job Descriptions	Document proposing new teller job description
1.3.1.4	Pay Scale	Document proposing new teller pay scale

     1.3.1.5   Advancement Requirements — Document proposing new requirements for teller advancement

1.3.2   FSR Solution Design — Document proposing solutions to FSR issues identified during analysis phase

     1.3.2.1   Hierarchy — Document proposing new hierarchical relationship of the FSR position

     1.3.2.2   Incentives — Document proposing new FSR incentive plan

     1.3.2.3   Job Descriptions — Document proposing new FSR job description

     1.3.2.4   Pay Scale — Document proposing new teller pay scale

     1.3.2.5   Advancement Requirements — Document proposing new requirements for FSR advancement

1.4   Restructuring Approval Documents — File of all signed branch network restructuring initiatives approval documents

1.4.1   Teller Restructuring Approval Document — File of all signed teller restructuring initiatives approval documents

     1.4.1.1   RBM Committee Approval Document — RBM signed teller restructuring initiatives approval document

     1.4.1.2   VP Branch Administration Approval Document — VP BA signed teller restructuring initiatives approval document

     1.4.1.3   EVP Branch Administration Approval Document — EVP BA signed teller restructuring initiatives approval document

     1.4.1.4   Human Resources Approval Document — HR signed teller restructuring initiatives approval document

1.4.2   FSR Restructuring Approval Document — File of all signed FSR restructuring initiatives approval documents

     1.4.2.1   RBM Committee Approval Document — RBM signed FSR restructuring initiatives approval document

     1.4.2.2   VP Branch Administration Approval Document — VP BA signed FSR restructuring initiatives approval document

     1.4.2.3   EVP Branch Administration Approval Document — EVP BA signed FSR restructuring initiatives approval document

     1.4.2.4   Human Resources Approval Document — HR signed FSR restructuring initiatives approval document

1.5	Restructuring Implementation Program	File of all branch network and Board of Directors restructuring implementation program meeting minutes
1.5.1	Teller Position Restructuring Implementation Program	File of all teller restructuring implementation program meeting minutes
1.5.1.1	Branch Manager Meeting	Teller restructuring implementation program meeting with branch manager minutes
1.5.1.2	Branch Meeting	Teller restructuring implementation program meeting with teller minutes
1.5.2	FSR Position Restructuring Implementation Program	File of all FSR restructuring implementation program meeting minutes
1.5.2.1	Branch Manager Meeting	FSR restructuring implementation program meeting with branch manager minutes
1.5.2.2	Branch Meeting	FSR restructuring implementation program meeting with FSRs minutes
1.5.3	Board of Directors Report	Teller and FSR restructuring implementation program meeting with BoD minutes

Industrial Construction Project

Graphical Work Breakdown Structure

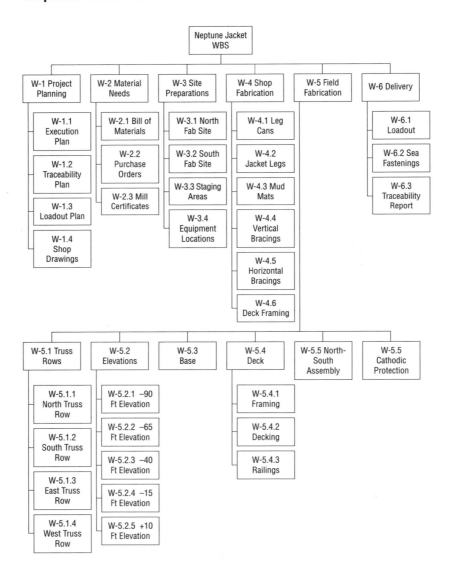

3 Resource Breakdown Structure

Managers have a long history of dividing anticipated project work into smaller and smaller parcels and graphically presenting the resulting structure. As with the WBS, this "breaking down" of the work facilitates management of the project's constituent elements in many ways. Similarly, during the very early stages of the project planning process, the project's in-house resources should be examined in an equally methodical manner in the process of creating the resource breakdown structure (RBS). If internal resources need to be augmented, this RBS must include project-specific resources that the manager needs to obtain from outside the organization. The RBS will greatly facilitate the resource assignments and scheduling in this project and in similar projects that use these resources.

An RBS differs from other human resource or budgeting classification methods because it applies directly to project management and not necessarily to, for example, cost accounting or personnel evaluations. The practice of formalizing the resource pool falls at point of the overlap between general management and project management.

An RBS classifies and catalogs the resources needed to accomplish project objectives. In many ways, the RBS is analogous to the WBS and claims similar advantages in improving communication, integration, planning, and estimating. As the WBS does for the deliverable elements of a project, the RBS provides a consistent framework for dividing the resources into small units for planning, estimating, and managing.

Figure 3-1 shows a schematic representation of the familiar WBS. The project deliverable, at the top, has been broken into many smaller deliverables. Figure 3-2 is the schematic representation of the RBS for the same project.

Rather than developing a new RBS for each project, the organization might choose to develop various RBS for families of projects. In some cases, the project manager might modify and use the resource structure that was previously prepared by those charged with accounting for the overall organizational resources. As project managers plan each new project, they might select only those portions of the common RBS that apply to the project.

In the few organizations that currently use variations of an enterprise RBS, the project manager can capitalize on organizational memory and use this structure to determine an accurate estimate for the cost of the resources needed for the project. Thus, project managers can plan the project with greater assurance of the reliability of the resource data. Regardless of how extensively it is used, the project or enterprise RBS must

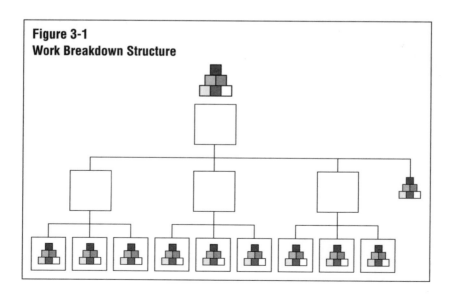

Figure 3-1
Work Breakdown Structure

Figure 3-2
Resource Breakdown Structure

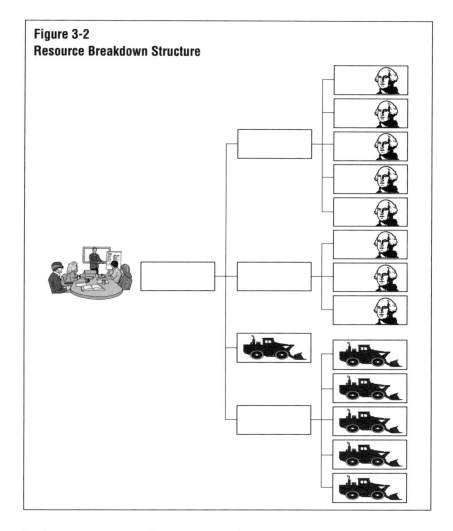

be kept current and accurate as far as content and costs of individual resources.

If the initial resource estimate of the project is prepared with reasonable accuracy, the proportional cost of each of the components of the project deliverable can be understood easily, even during the early stages of the project, when the structure and values may not be exceptionally accurate. The project estimate will be easy to review and improve as more information becomes available. As the almost inevitable changes of scope occur, further modifications to the estimate can be made formally, easily, and clearly.

Equally important, every change to the project cost can be justified and defended with detailed data. The incidence of scope creep can be significantly reduced, or even eliminated, when a detailed bottom-up estimate is prepared using a deliverable-oriented WBS and an appropriate RBS.

RBS DEVELOPMENT

An enterprise-oriented, or even a project-oriented, RBS is not used to plan any particular project. Instead, it tabulates the resources available to, or needed in, certain type of projects, or even for a specific project. Developing the RBS starts with dividing the pool of resources into entities specific enough so that this structure can be used as a catalog for resources that are necessary to deliver the project WBS elements.

Developing an RBS involves grouping all resources into approximately three to nine categories in Level One. Then, each of the Level One items is subdivided as described for the WBS in Chapter 2. Consistency in the division bases remains a crucial component of the structure. Ideally, the rationale for dividing one level from the next should be consistent across all elements and branches of the RBS, but at a minimum the division basis at any juncture must be the same for all children of the same parent.

The process continues until discrete, manageable resource items have been identified. A useful guide here is to keep dividing the resource pool until the lowest-level items reflect the level of resource detail that is of interest to the estimators and schedulers, stopping short of naming individuals. The RBS can be presented graphically, in a tabular fashion or using indented text.

Again, the level of detail at the lowest level of the RBS varies among companies and project managers. The nature of the resource pool and its administrative environment determine the depths of the levels. Notwithstanding, reasonable consistency must be maintained in the degree of detail of the lowest-level elements from all of the branches. For example, in a listing of materials for a construction project, if two resource branches end with nails and motors, respectively, there is not a consistency in significance of the individual resources.

Some high-priority projects may have limitless resources, for example, as many CAD operators, contract officers, or safety engineers as the project needs. On the other hand, if some of the resources are limited, the RBS may identify those resources. For example, it would mention that 14 civil engineers are available for a new project—or 2 cranes, 35 brick layers, 4 programmers, 3 photographers, and so forth.

Sometimes complications arise when the client provides some combination of equipment, funding, and personnel. Although in such cases the detailed solution varies depending on the nature of the project and the priorities of the organizations involved, the most logical and thorough approach would be to list all of the necessary project resources in the RBS—and in the estimate—regardless of how they will be funded. Once the total project cost estimate is prepared, the client-furnished equipment and labor costs can be subtracted from the resources requested by the project manager or the contractor.

Several examples of RBS are presented at the end of this chapter.

THE PRIMARY DIVISION BASES

The best, although not necessarily the only, lines of demarcation among the elements at the first level of the RBS are:

- People (labor)

- Tools, machinery

- Materials and installed equipment

- Fees, licenses.

The labor category is sometimes referred to as people resources. Depending on organizational and personal preferences, people are grouped by skill categories, professional disciplines, and work functions, in addition to being grouped by location, account, and organization. The RBS should list all possible human resources, regardless of their physical location, administrative attachment, or contractual circumstances. Doing so will facilitate implementation of plans that might involve assigning personnel or allocating funds from different organizational entities.

Figure 3-3 shows the categorization of human resources along organizational lines. Figure 3-4 shows the RBS for the stack monitor project described in the WBS chapter.

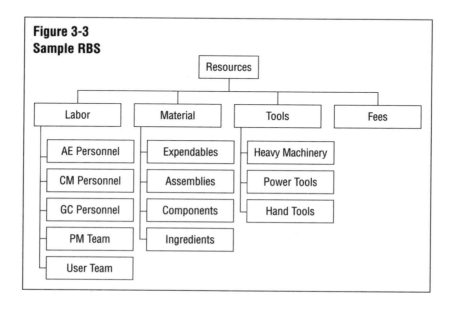

Figure 3-3
Sample RBS

Figure 3-4
RBS for Stack Project

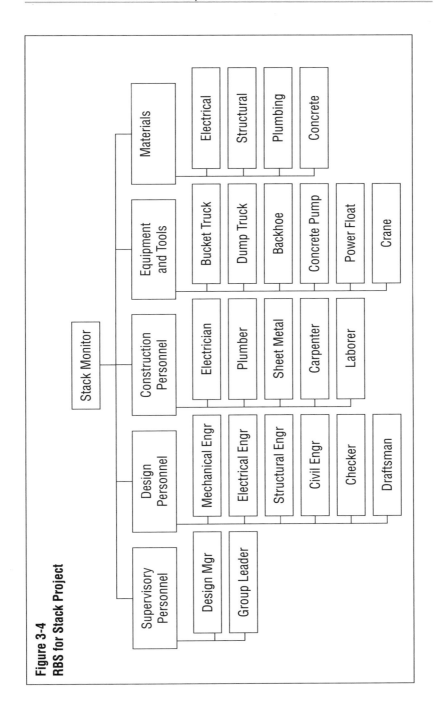

Tools and machinery are those physical items the project team members need to perform their duties successfully. Thus, when the project ends, the project team will remove the tools and machinery from the project environment. Examples of items in this category are testing hardware, hand tools, hardware to install project deliverables, and computers to monitor and evaluate the installation process. These items are usually leased or rented. Sometimes, purchasing this type of resource can be more cost-effective for lengthy projects, even though ultimately these resources still will be removed from the project site upon successful completion of the project.

For planning and cost estimating purposes, sometimes the leasing agencies roll the wages of the operator into the rental fee of the equipment. Consequently, when tools and machinery are rented or leased, some organizations treat the operator as an integral part of the physical equipment. This practice blurs the line between the human and physical resources and should therefore be used sparingly and only when it clearly makes sense to do it that way.

Installed materials and equipment are purchased for the project and ultimately are integrated and embedded into the project deliverable. Examples include fiber-optic cables, furniture, tape drives, monitoring equipment, pumps, ducts, and computers. Computers are one of several categories of items that might be listed under tools and estimated with a time-based unit, because some of them will be used by the project team during project implementation. Yet they also might be listed under embedded equipment and estimated as each unit because some of them will be embedded in the deliverable.

Fees and licenses refer to those cost items that do not involve any implementation or installation but are required to execute the project. Examples include insurance policies, bond agreements, permit fees, legal fees, license charges, and taxes. Fees can be divided by type or by cost.

Ideally, the project manager should plan, estimate, and manage all tasks and their respective resources independent of where the resources reside, administratively or physically. If a human resource is from an outside organization and the project manager intends to hire that person for an individual task, then that task and its associated resources should not be regarded as part of the project at hand. If the project manager does not have managerial authority over a certain resource, then this project manager has no major influence in the use of the resource. In these cases, the resource and the resulting product are aptly named "outsourced."

Equipment, supplies, tools, and material can be categorized by size, function, cost, or technical area. Aside from these general guidelines, equipment, materials, and fees are highly dependent on the discipline of the project and must be dealt with on a project-by-project basis. However, categorizing people is common to all projects, and people are the most important resource in any project. Generally 40–50 percent of the cost of construction and industrial projects is attributable to labor costs. The cost of human resources is approximately 60–90 percent of the cost of systems and software development projects (Anonymous[2] 1999; Anonymous[5] 1999; Vidger & Kark 1994).

LOWER-LEVEL DIVISION BASES FOR PEOPLE RESOURCES

The level of detail with which an RBS defines a human resource depends on the organization, the project, and to some extent the individual project manager. That stated, the transition from one people-resource RBS level to the next should occur based on one of the following:

- Administrative unit

- Charge code of account

- Physical location

- Credential (in a particular discipline)

- Work function

- Position title

- Skill level.

Organizational managers sometimes divide resources on the basis of their administrative affiliations, such as Company A, Contractor X, or Organization D. In other cases, they might prefer to catalog the resources into groups based on physical location, especially as it relates to proximity to the project site (e.g., people resources from Los Angeles, Boston, southern plants, or western contractors). Normally, the first three bases are more appropriate for higher levels of the RBS, while credential, function, title, and skill are more appropriate bases for lower levels.

The credential-discipline basis is used when resources need to be identified by their degree specializations, certifications, or other recognized credentials. A work function basis is used when managers must know workers' functions, independent of their credentials. Position title basis is required when, independent of their credentials or job functions, people's places in the organizational hierarchy determine their duties in the project. Examples of such divisions are contract officers, program directors, department chiefs, and divisional VPs.

Occasionally it is appropriate to classify project personnel by their degree of effectiveness and skill (e.g., expert, skilled, semi-skilled). Naturally, the skill designation should always be used in conjunction with credential or function designations, and not title. Therefore, when credential and function designations are used, a next level of resource can be created. For example, if the lowest level of an RBS branch is, say, programmers, then the next level can be created by indicating the skill level of this resource (i.e., competent, skilled, and expert).

Again, for best results, one must maintain a reasonable level of consistency in grouping the resources. For example, whether labor items are categorized by degree, job title, or job function, the categorization should be consistent across all labor items at that level of the RBS. The RBS should not be extended to the named individuals in the organization because that will confuse the resource allocation for a project. This practice would be appropriate only in exceptionally rare organizations where the resource profile is absolutely fixed and there is no likelihood of changes, and therefore all project planning is conducted on a resource-constrained basis, and with named resources.

Figures 3-5 and 3-6 illustrate the WBS and RBS for a systems development project. These figures show the similarities and differences between these two structures. The structures are similar in the sense that they have a logical basis of breakdown from a broader viewpoint to the most detailed. They are complementary in that WBS is client-centric and the RBS is team-centric. The WBS shows the results of the project as the client will see them, whereas the RBS highlights the means by which the team will implement the project. To be more specific, the WBS will describe the deliverable, whereas the RBS will describe the resources to be used in crafting that specific deliverable.

NOMENCLATURE, DIMENSIONS, AND UNITS

The term "resource" refers to anything that will cost money to obtain and is necessary to complete the project (e.g., labor, equipment, licenses, taxes). Money is not a resource in this breakdown structure, but it is used as a common denomination of all resources. Money represents the primary means by which resources are provided.

For example, consider that for internal projects, money is often not the exchange medium. Although resources such as worker hours or equipment may then be granted directly, the project manager should still regard them as resources to be listed in the RBS—resources whose cost will be absorbed by the enterprise, implicitly or explicitly. Even for external projects, money should not be treated as a resource; it is the means by which the client buys the project deliverable, and in turn it

Figure 3-5
WBS Industrial System Development

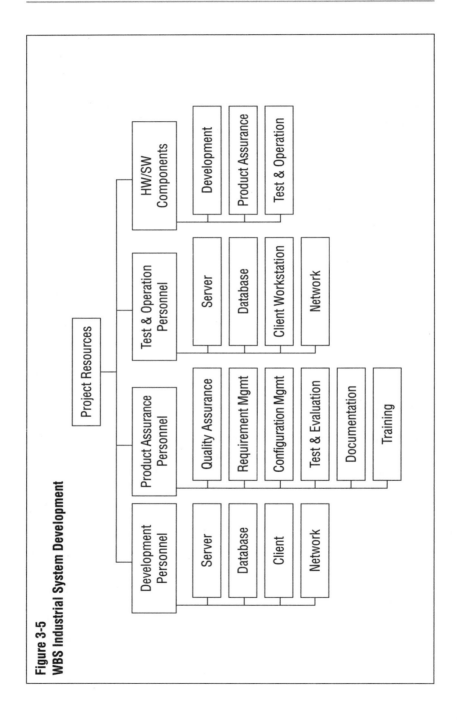

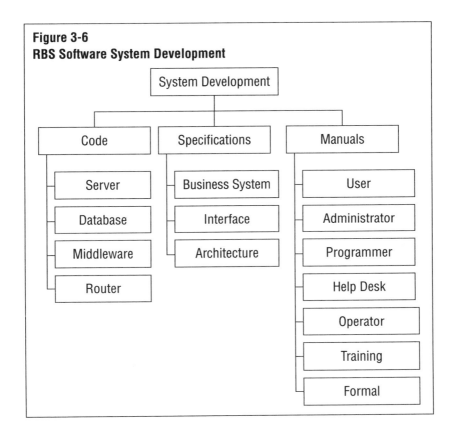

Figure 3-6
RBS Software System Development

is the means by which the contractor buys all of the resources needed to complete the project.

Because workers are paid for their effort, albeit differently in internal and external projects, they represent an expense to the enterprise, and their efforts add up to the project cost. Therefore, resource effort should be viewed as equivalent to cost. These issues must be kept in mind even in organizations in which the cost of the project is reported only for materials and equipment, and possibly service, that must be purchased from outside the organization.

The RBS explicitly contains both the unit of measurement for each resource (e.g., foot, pound, cubic yard, equipment hour, labor hour) and the cost of a single unit of the resource (e.g., $200 per programmer hour, $10,000 per equipment hour). Discrete items that, individually or in groups, get consumed or used entirely in a project can be measured as "each," for example, installed motors, doors, computers, and hard disks. The RBS may list either direct costs or total costs, i.e., overhead. However, all resource costs should be listed using identical or consistent measurement units, either with or without overhead, and not a blend of the two. Blending those resource costs that include overhead with those that do not completely destroys the accuracy and utility of the RBS, and ultimately that of the resulting project estimate.

The measurement unit for all time-related elements can be hours, days, months, or years, but the chosen unit should appear in all appropriate quantities (unless the numbers become unreasonably large or inordinately small). The same statement can be made about all other dimensions and combinations of dimensions involved in the project, such as length (inches, feet, yards, centimeters, meters, kilometers) or volume (gallons, cubic yards, cubic centimeters, cubic meters).

Consistency is particularly important for time-related items. If the same units of time are not used in all of the RBS elements, then the link between the RBS and the schedule always must include a conversion schema that develops one unit of duration measurement for all elements in the schedule. As a reminder of the importance of this consistency in the measurement units (and many other consistencies), consider the example of the Mars Climate Orbiter, which failed in September 1999 because one navigating group worked in English (FPS, foot-pound-second) units and the other in metric (SI, meter-kilogram-second) units (Kerr 1999). A much tighter consistency than this minimum requirement of working in the same unit system would be better.

The word "rate" means some quantity measured per unit of time (e.g., a worker's cost rate could be measured in dollars per hour). If one needed to discuss the expense of a single item (e.g., a can of paint), the cost would be described not as a rate but simply as so many dollars per unit; the unit may be called "each."

"Effort" is the product of workers and time, measured in worker hours, worker days, worker months, or worker years. At any given point in the project, the effort divided by the appropriate unit of time gives the number of workers. For example, if a project requires an effort of 100 worker years, completion over a year's duration would require 100 workers; to be completed in six months (i.e., 0.5 years), 200 workers would be needed.

This illustration, however, ignores the effect of compression and expansion on the cost. It also ignores the effects of varying skill level, because we are assuming that all workers have a similar skill level and do similar work, which may not be correct. The number of resources that would be present during the execution of a given task, or the "instantaneous" worker need, will be called the "resource intensity" for the task. This intensity will become the input to the schemas by which resource loading histograms are prepared, which in turn would flag "overloading" of resources. The remedy for resource overload is either hiring more resources for that specific time frame or avoiding it by virtue of a schedule expansion, commonly referred to as "resource leveling."

Units must be retained in such arithmetic, whether explicitly or implicitly, so that the translation from effort to cost occurs through the cost rate per worker (e.g., worker hours multiplied by dollars per hour per worker yields dollars). Figures 3-7 and 3-8 show a schematic representation of estimating the cost of using personnel or equipment over some duration. If three workers are used for four days, we have used 12 worker days (see Figure 3-7). Then, multiplying by the cost rate yields the cost for that effort. Calculating the cost of equipment is similar except that now the effort is measured in equipment days (see Figure 3-8).

"Estimates" are made through this conversion. Although the objective may be to estimate cost, the first, often hidden (and

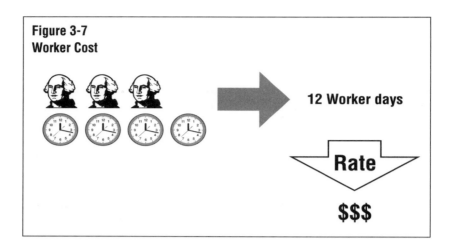

Figure 3-7
Worker Cost

12 Worker days

Rate

$$$

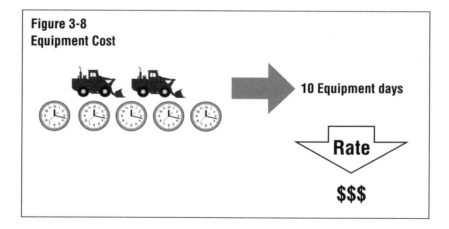

Figure 3-8
Equipment Cost

10 Equipment days

Rate

$$$

sometimes skipped) step is to estimate the effort. A conceptual estimate of an element can initially be the total cost, but ultimately detailed cost estimates must be based on estimates of the quantity of resources.

Developing an RBS requires an analog of the logic and philosophy used in developing a WBS. An RBS categorizes and tabulates the resource pool that is available, or should be available, to the project. An RBS will provide a systematic and formalized tool for calculating the cost of individual resources that are needed for each task of the project. Summarizing these costs across all resources will result in detailed estimates for the project on a resource-by-resource basis. Additionally, summarizing such costs across WBS elements will provide cost details for each of the project's deliverables.

The availability of detailed resource costs will significantly improve the accuracy of the estimate. More important, the RBS will facilitate analysis of the changes to the project's cost as a result of the inevitable changes in the project's environment.

Resource Breakdown Structure Examples

Home Building Project

Hardware Design Project

Health Services Project

Bank Data Conversion Software Project

Wireless Communications Project

Branch Network Restructuring Project

Industrial Construction Project

Home Building Project

Resource Breakdown Structure

Resource	Unit of Measure	Cost ($)
1.0 Personnel		
1.1 Design		
1.1.1 Mechanical engineers	Hour	60
1.1.2 Electrical engineers	Hour	60
1.1.3 Civil engineers	Hour	60
1.1.4 Architects	Hour	60
1.1.5 Project controls engineers	Hour	60
1.1.6 Drafters	Hour	38
1.2 Construction Management		
1.2.1 Project manager	Hour	100
1.2.2 Project engineers	Hour	60
1.2.3 Superintendents	Hour	60
1.2.4 Technical clerks	Hour	30
1.3 Skilled Labor		
1.3.1 Foremen	Hour	55.00
1.3.2 Welders/pipefitters	Hour	47.91
1.3.3 Electricians	Hour	45.40
1.3.4 Painters	Hour	42.02
1.3.5 Carpenters	Hour	47.85
1.3.6 Plumbers	Hour	47.53
1.3.7 Drywall installers	Hour	41.10
1.3.8 Laborers	Hour	34.23
1.4 Support Personnel		
1.4.1 Procurement managers	Hour	40
1.4.2 Materials managers (warehousing)	Hour	40
1.4.3 Accountants	Hour	55
1.4.4 Safety engineers	Hour	40
1.4.5 Security personnel	Hour	30
1.4.6 Medical personnel	Hour	55
1.4.7 Administrative assistants	Hour	40
2.0 Equipment		
2.1 Major		
2.1.1 Crane (15 ton, includes operator)	Day	800
2.1.2 Bulldozers (140 horsepower)	Day	612
2.1.3 Backhoes (3/8 cubic yard)	Day	195
2.1.4 Dump trucks (10 cubic yard)	Day	230
2.1.5 Front-end loader (2 cubic yard)	Day	301

Resource	Unit of Measure	Cost ($)
2.2 Minor		
2.2.1 Welding machine (200 ampere)	Day	54
2.2.2 Air compressors		
(100 cubic feet/minute)	Day	90
2.2.3 Generators (15 KW, diesel)	Day	217
2.2.4 Portable lights	Day	3
2.2.5 Spray painters (8 cubic feet/minute)	Day	50
2.2.6 Scaffold	Day	20
2.3 Support		
2.3.1 Office trailers	Day	12
2.3.2 Garbage dumpsters (40 cubic yards)	Each removal	215
2.3.3 Portable toilets	Day	2
2.3.4 Computer with printer	Each	1500
3.0 Tools		
3.1 Hand tools	Each	15
3.2 Ladders	Each	40
3.3 Pneumatic tools (nail guns, etc.)	Each	150
3.4 Electric tools (saws, etc.)	Each	100
4.0 Materials		
4.1 Civil/Architectural		
4.1.1 Concrete (ready-mix, delivered by truck)	Cubic yard	64
4.1.2 Lumber (2" by 4", 8' long)	Each	4
4.1.3 Paint	Gallon	23
4.1.4 Drywall (1/2" thick, 4' by 8' panels)	Each	6.05
4.1.5 Insulation (1" thick)	Pound	0.46
4.1.6 Misc. (nails, nuts, bolts, etc.)	Pound	1.50
4.2 Electrical		
4.2.1 Wire (copper, #4 gauge)	Foot	0.55
4.2.2 Switches (3-way lighting)	Each	3.86
4.2.3 Air conditioner (room)	Each	200
4.2.4 Lighting fixtures (ceiling)	Each	75
4.3 Mechanical		
4.3.1 Pipe and fitting (2", stainless steel)	Foot	9.86
4.3.2 Air ducts (8", fiberglass, insulated)	Foot	2.68
4.3.3 Furnace (gas, 4 ton, 75,000 BTU)	Each	400

Hardware Design Project

Resource Breakdown Structure

Resource	Unit of Measure	Supply Limit	Cost ($)
Personnel			
1.1. Design Engineers			
1.1.1 Design Manager			
1.1.1.1 Senior level	Yr	1	275,000
1.1.2. Circuit Design Engineers			
1.1.2.1. Analog			
1.1.2.1.1. Principal level	Yr	1	255,000
1.1.2.1.2. Staff level	Yr	2	225,000
1.1.2.1.3. Sr. level	Yr	1	200,000
1.1.2.1.4. Intermediate level	Yr	3	167,500
1.1.2.1.5. Engineer level	Yr	1	145,000
1.1.2.2. Digital			
1.1.2.2.1. Staff level	Yr	1	200,000
1.1.2.2.2. Sr. level	Yr	1	185,000
1.1.2.2.3. Intermediate level	Yr	2	160,000
1.1.3. Mask Design Engineers			
1.1.3.1. Sr. level	Yr	1	130,000
1.1.3.2. Intermediate level	Yr	1	115,000
1.1.3.3. Engineer level	Yr	1	97,500
1.2. CAE Engineers (Computer Automated Engineering)			
1.2.1. Staff level	Yr	1	200,000
1.2.2. Sr. Level	Yr	1	185,000
1.3. ESD Engineers (Electro-Static Discharge)			
1.3.1. Principal level	Yr	1	210,000
1.3.2. Staff level	Yr	2	182,500
1.4. Applications Engineers			
1.4.1. Principal level	Yr	1	165,000
1.4.2. Intermediate level	Yr	1	125,500
1.4.3. Engineer level	Yr	1	105,000
1.5. Product Engineers			
1.5.1. Staff level	Yr	1	150,000
1.5.2. Sr. level	Yr	1	135,500
1.6. FA Engineers (Failure Analysis)			
1.6.1. Principal level	Yr	1	160,000
1.6.2. Sr. level	Yr	1	130,000
1.6.3. Intermediate level	Yr	1	115,500
1.7. Project Management			
1.7.1. Staff level	Yr	3	140,000

Resource	Unit of Measure	Supply Limit	Cost ($)
1.8. System Administration			
1.8.1. Staff level	Yr	1	130,000
1.8.2. Intermediate level	Yr	2	155,500
2 Tools			
2.1 Computers			
2.1.1 Unix	5 payments, yearly	17	4,000
2.1.2 PC	5 payments, yearly	15	500
2.2 Projector	5 payments, yearly	3	850
2.3 Plotter	5 payments, yearly	1	2000
2.4 Printer			
2.4.1 Color	5 payments, yearly	1	1,100
2.4.2 B/W	5 payments, yearly	1	625
2.5 Test Boards			
2.5.1 AC board fab run	each	Unlimited	5,000
2.5.2 DC board fab run	each	Unlimited	4,000
2.5.3 Jitter board fab run	each	Unlimited	5,000
2.5.4 Sockets	each	Unlimited	1,500
2.5.5 Application board	each	Unlimited	2,000
2.6 Test Equipment			
2.6.1 AC setup	5 payments, yearly	2	60,000
2.6.2 DC setup	5 payments, yearly	1	45,000
3 Licenses			
3.1 Software			
3.1.1 Cadence	yearly	25	20,000
3.1.2 Microsoft project	yearly	3	500

All personnel (Section 1.0) available in this project environment are salaried employees. A small amount of the fringe benefit may vary year to year, but for this assignment it is considered constant. Depending on the software utilized in creating the project schedule in later assignments, care must be given to make sure that an overtime rate is assigned as $0.00. The personnel resources are not able to receive overtime pay. In order to indicate this, all personnel rates are as given as cost/year. The personnel are first grouped by function. The lowest function level is then grouped by job title.

Most of the tools available in this project environment (Section 2.0, excluding section 2.5) are capitalized purchases. The tools are depreciated in a straight-line manner over five years. The depreciation value per year is included in the RBS for cost purposes. In order to allocate cost for the RBS it is assumed that the tools have been recently purchased; therefore, current book value is equal to purchase price. The tools are grouped by logical segments. Some segments are then further grouped by type.

The test boards and sockets (Section 2.5) are generated and charged on a per-project basis if needed. The boards are purchased from a vendor and processed as a sheet. The vendor can yield up to six boards but guarantees a yield of four. If the yield is higher than four, the charge does not change.

Health Services Project

Resource Breakdown Structure

Resource	Unit of Measurement	Cost/ Price ($)
Outpatient Occupational Therapy Center		
1 Expertise and Skills		
1.1 Occupational Therapy Services		
1 1.1.1 Registered occupational therapist	Hour	27.50
1 1.1.2 Certified occupational therapy assistant	Hour	17.00
1 1.1.3 Occupational therapy counselor	Hour	22.00
1.1.1.4 Registered nurse	Hour	23.00
1.1.1.5 Medical assistant	Hour	10.00
1.2 Medical Assistant		
1 1.2.1 Nursing aide	Hour	10.00
1.1.2.2 Home health aide	Hour	10.00
1.1.2.3 Social worker	Hour	20.00
1.1.2.4 Financial advisor for patients	Hour	14.00
1.1.2.5 Equipment maintenance specialist	Hour	12.00
1.1.2.6 Maid and housekeeper	Hour	13.00
1.1.2.7 Security guard	Hour	12.00
1.3 Administrative and management services		
1.1.3.1 Project manager	Hour	30.00
1.1.3.2 Administrative assistant	Hour	17.00
1.1.3.3 Receptionist and information desk clerk	Hour	13.00
1.1.3.4 Accountant	Hour	17.50
2 Equipment and Material		
2.1 Occupational Therapy Equipment		
1.2.1.1 Diagnostic equipment		
2.1.1.1 Physical evaluation kit	Each	500.00
2.1.1.2 Neurological evaluation kit	Each	230.00
2.1.1.3 Cognitive evaluation kit	Each	225.00
2.1.1.4 Pediatrlc evaluation kit	Each	750.00
2.1.2 Therapeutic Equipments		
2.1.2.1 Physical therapeutic equipment	Set	2,200.00
2.1.2.2 Neurological therapeutic equipment	Set	1,000.00
2.1.2.3 Cognitive therapeutic equipment	Set	1,500.00
2.1.2.4 Pediatric therapeutic equipment	Set	1,400.00
2.1.3 Rehabilitative Equipments		
2.1.3.1 Physical rehabilitative equipment	Set	3,000.00
2.1.3.2 Neurological rehabilitative equipment	Set	1,000.00
2.1.3.3 Cognitive rehabilitative equipment	Set	750.00
2.1.3.4 Pediatric rehabilitative equipment	Set	1,000.00

Resource	Unit of Measurement	Cost/ Price ($)
2.2 Facility Equipment		
2.1 Furniture		
2.2.1.1 Chairs	Each	75.00
		150.00
2.2.1.3 Information desks	Each	250.00
2.2.1.4 Beds	Each	750.00
2.2.1.5 Storage closets	Each	75.00
2.2.2 Housekeeping		
2.2.2.1 Kitchen equipment	Set	1,500.00
2.2.2.2 Restroom equipment	Set	1,500.00
2.2.2.3 Cleaning equipment	Set	850.00
2.2.2.4 Security equipment	Set	1,200.00
2.2.3 Entertainment for Patients and Caretakers		
2.2.3.1 Television set	Each	500.00
2.2.3.2 Radio and music system	Each	200.00
2.2.3.3 Books and magazines	Set	250.00
2.2.3.4 Children's games	Set	250.00
2.3 Office Equipment		
2.3.1 Telephone sets	Each	200.00
2.3.2 Fax machine	Each	300.00
2.3.3 Computers	Each	2,000.00
2.3.4 Stationery	Set	1,200.00
3.1 Licenses		
3.1.1 Business	Monthly Payment	50.00
3.1.2 Registered occupational therapist	Monthly Payment for each OTR	40.00
3.1.3 Certified occupational therapy assistant	Monthly Payment for each COTA	40.00
3.1.4 Registered nurse	Monthly Payment for each RN	25.00
3.1.5 Software	Monthly Payment for all the software	20.00
3.2 Insurances		
3.2.1 Business	Monthly Payment	150.00
3.2.2 Registered occupational therapist	Monthly Payment for each OTR	250.00
3.2.3 Certified occupational therapy assistant	Monthly Payment for each COTA	150.00
3.2.4 Registered nurse	Monthly Payment for each RN	200.00
3.2.5 Warranties and insurance on equipment	Monthly Payment for all the equipment	10.00

Resource	Unit of Measurement	Cost/ Price ($)
3.3 Office Space Rent and Utilities	Monthly Payments	3,000.00
3.4 Consulting and Contracting Fees		
3.4.1 Architect	Hour	25.00
3.4.2 Interior decorators	Hour	100.00
3.4.3 Business lawyers	Hour	25.00
3.4.4 Security system installers	Hour	15.00
3.4.5 Exterior decorators	Hour	35.00

The prices are derived from the websites of Salary.com, American Occupational Therapists' Association, Occupational Therapist.com, the Washington Post, and Office Depot.

Bank Data Conversion Software Project

Resource Breakdown Structure

The following represents the pool of resources available for assignment to the project. Note that any project entry requirement costs (e.g., network infrastructure to support remote work) are assumed by the client to be external to the project and are not enumerated below.

All internal rates identified are valid for, and are guaranteed through, the calendar year 2003, and are valid for use of these resources in any geography in which the company operates. These rates are internally published and fully burdened and therefore already include many of the incidental ongoing expenses of the practice, such as home office support, cell phones, laptop computer, general software, office supplies, etc. Note that within a given discipline, the band level or title reflects the relative skill level of the individual in that discipline. The rates for each band level are identified in the final table.

Contractor rates, where used, are also fully burdened and apply to the same time period and geography, and are the rates negotiated with vendors approved by the purchasing organization.

As XYZ is so large, for all practical purposes, there is no limit to the availability of any of these skills.

Category	Sub-Category	Description	Unit	Cost/Unit
People	Project Mgmt	Practice Executive	Hour	Band D
		Principal	Hour	Band 10
		Project Office Manager	Hour	Band 10
		Sr. Conversion Manager	Hour	Band 09
		Advisory Conversion Manager	Hour	Band 08
		Sr. Test Manager	Hour	Band 09
		Advisory Test Manager	Hour	Band 08
		Test Coordinator	Hour	Band 07
		Project Assistant	Hour	Band 07
		Project Administrator	Hour	Band 06
	Methodology	Sr. Methodology Advocate	Hour	Band 09
		Advisory Methodlogy Advocate	Hour	Band 08
	Business Analysts	Sr. BA—Banking	Hour	Band 09
		Adv. BA—Banking	Hour	Band 08
		Assoc. BA—Banking	Hour	Band 07
		Contracted Adv. BA—Banking	Hour	$55
		Contracted Assoc. BA—Banking	Hour	$40

Category	Sub-Category	Description	Unit	Cost/Unit
	Admin	Contract Manager	Hour	Band 07
		Admin Support ("Secretarial")	Hour	Band 05
		Contracted Admin Support	Hour	$20
		Sr. SW Librarian	Hour	Band 07
		Associate SW Librarian	Hour	Band 06
		Staffing Manager	Hour	Band 08
		Quality Assurance Manager	Hour	Band 08
	Programming	Sr. Conversion Architect	Hour	Band 09
		Advisory Conversion Architect	Hour	Band 08
		Sr. Application Architect	Hour	Band 09
		Advisory Application Architect	Hour	Band 08
		Sr. Programmer—Host Cobol	Hour	Band 09
		Advisory Programmer—Host Cobol	Hour	Band 08
		Associate Programmer—Host Cobol	Hour	Band 07
		Sr. Programmer—Java & WebSphere	Hour	Band 09
		Advisory Programmer—Java & WebSphere	Hour	Band 08
		Associate Programmer—Java & WebSphere	Hour	Band 07
		Apprentice Programmer (general)	Hour	Band 06
		Contract Programmer— Sr. Host Cobol	Hour	$55
		Contract Programmer— Adv. Host Cobol	Hour	$45
		Contract Programmer—Entry Cobol	Hour	$25
		Contract Programmer— Sr. Java & WS	Hour	$75
		Contract Programmer— Adv. Java & WS	Hour	$55
		Contract Programmer—Entry Java	Hour	$35
	Consultants	Sr. Consultant—Banking	Hour	Band 09
		Adv. Consultant—Banking	Hour	Band 08
		Assoc. Consultant—Banking	Hour	Band 07
		Apprentice Consultant (general)	Hour	Band 06
Travel	To Client Site	Local Resource (est)	Person-Day	$10
		Remote Resource (est)	Person-Trip-Week	$1800
	International Work Permit	Total Processing	Person-Year	$1000
	Media Delivery	Local Delivery	Event	$200
		Remote Delivery	Event	$2000

Category	Sub-Category	Description	Unit	Cost/Unit
Fees, Licenses	Conversion Process Software	Gladstone Limited License— Large installation	One	$60,000
		Gladstone Limited License— Medium installation	One	$40,000
		Gladstone Limited License— Small installation	One	$25,000
		Gladstone Permanent License— Large Enterprise	One	$180,000
		Gladstone Permanent License— Medium Enterprise	One	$120,000
		Gladstone Permanent License— Small Enterprise	One	$75,000
	Meeting Rooms	Conf Room—very large (40–75 persons, projector, etc)	Hour	$350
		Conf Room—Large (20–40 persons, projector, etc.)	Hour	$250
		Conf Room—Medium (10–20 persons, projector, etc)	Hour	$100
		Conf Room—Small (3–10 persons, no projector)	Hour	$30
	Catered Lunch	Deli style	Person	$8

Band Level Costs

Band Level	Cost/Hour
5	$60
6	$79
7	$91
8	$125
9	$165
10	$230
D	$280

Wireless Communications Project

Resource Breakdown Structure

Shared Hub Operations *(cost is before overhead)*	*Measure*	*Quantity*	*Price ($)*
1.0 Personnel			
1.1 Operations Management			
1.1.1 Vice President	Hr.	1	72.12
1.1.2 Director of Operations	Hr.	1	60.10
1.2 Hub Infrastructure			
1.2.1 Network Planning			
1.2.1.1 Manager	Hr.	1	44.23
1.2.1.2 Technician	Hr.	11	36.41
1.2.1.3 Contractor	Hr.	2	85.00
1.2.2 Space Segment Utilization			
1.2.2.1 Manager	Hr.	1	44.23
1.2.2.2 Technician	Hr.	1	36.41
1.2.3 Capital Management			
1.2.3.1 Manager	Hr.	1	44.23
1.2.3.2 Technician	Hr.	2	36.41
1.2.4 Radio Frequency Terminal Maintenance			
1.3.1 Manager	Hr.	1	43.27
1.3.2 Technician	Hr.	2	24.04
1.3 Los Angeles Hub Operations			
1.3.1 Hub Manager	Hr.	1	30.30
1.3.2 Hub Technician	Hr.	7	24.24
1.3.3 Contractors	Hr.	1	44.00
1.4 Minneapolis Hub Operations			
1.4.1 Hub Manager	Hr.	1	29.40
1.4.2 Hub Technician	Hr.	7	23.52
1.4.3 Contractors	Hr.	4	18.00
1.5 Detroit Hub Operations			
1.5.1 Hub Manager	Hr.	1	30.70
1.5.2 Hub Technician	Hr.	23	24.56
1.5.3 Contractors	Hr.	6	23.00
1.6 Germantown Hub Operations			
1.6.1 Hub Manager	Hr.	1	28.63
1.6.2 Hub Technician	Hr.	7	22.90
1.6.3 Contractors	Hr.	4	23.76
1.7 Engineering Support			
1.7.1 Engineering Manager	Hr.	1	40.75
1.7.2 Engineer	Hr.	13	32.60

Shared Hub Operations
(cost is before overhead)   *Measure   Quantity   Price ($)*

			Measure	Quantity	Price ($)
2.0	Equipment				
	2.1	DirecWay Equipment			
		2.1.1 DirecPC Enterprise Network Operation Center	ea.	13	150,000.00
		2.1.2 Internet Protocol Gateway	ea.	35	6,300.00
		2.1.3 Statistical Control Processor	ea.	13	10,000.00
	2.2	ISBN Equipment			
		2.2.1 ISBN Netgroup	ea.	49	150,000.00
		2.2.2 SLIM (Super Lan Interface Module)	ea.	369	1,500.00
		2.2.3 Baseband Channel Demodulator	ea.	632	4,500.00
		2.2.4 Alpha Illuminet	ea.	43	7,000.00
		2.2.5 Statistical Control Processor	ea.	49	10,000.00
	2.3	Backhaul Equipment			
		2.3.1 HubSide Routers	ea.	169	4,000.00
	2.4	Tools			
		2.4.1 Lan Sniffer	ea.	4	20,000.00
		2.4.2 Spectrum Analyzer	ea.	8	35,000.00
	2.5	Radio Frequency Terminal Equipment			
		2.5.1 Antenna	ea.	9	250,000.00
		2.5.2 UP/Down Converters	ea.	18	8,000.00
		2.5.3 High Power Amplifier	ea.	18	75,000.00
3.0	Satellites				
	3.1	Galaxy 10			
		3.1.1 36 Mhz Transponder Capacity	month		150,000.00
		3.1.2 54 Mhz Transponder Capacity	month		180,000.00
	3.2	Galaxy 11			
		3.2.1 36 Mhz Transponder Capacity	month		150,000.00
		3.2.2 54 Mhz Transponder Capacity	month		180,000.00
	3.3	Galaxy 3R			
		3.3.1 36 Mhz Transponder Capacity	month		150,000.00
		3.3.2 54 Mhz Transponder Capacity	month		180,000.00
	3.4	PamAmSat 3R			
		3.4.1 36 Mhz Transponder Capacity	month		150,000.00
		3.4.2 54 Mhz Transponder Capacity	month		180,000.00
	3.5	Telestar 5			
		3.5.1 36 Mhz Transponder Capacity	month		150,000.00
		3.5.2 54 Mhz Transponder Capacity	month		180,000.00

Branch Network Restructuring Project

Resource Breakdown Structure

	Units of Measure	Quantity Available for Br. Adm. Project	Cost/ Price ($)*
1.0 Personnel			
1.1 Executive			
1.1.1 Director	Hour	16	$177.00
1.1.2 Chairman of the Board	Hour	1	$146.00
1.1.3 Chief Executive Officer	Hour	1	$162.00
1.1.4 Executive Vice President	Hour	2	$71.00
1.1.5 Executive Secretary	Hour	2	$19.00
1.2 Branch Administration			
1.2.1 Vice President	Hour		$32.00
1.2.2 Assistant Vice President	Hour		$22.00
1.2.3 Trainer	Hour		$15.00
1.2.4 Administrative Assistant	Hour		$12.00
1.2.5 Quality Control Clerk	Hour		$13.00
1.3 Branch Network			
1.3.1 Manager	Hour	11	$19.00
1.3.2 Assistant Manager	Hour	8	$16.00
1.3.3 Senior Financial Service Representative	Hour	9	$14.00
1.3.4 Financial Service Representative	Hour	5	$13.00
1.3.5 Head Teller	Hour	11	$13.00
1.3.6 Assistant Head Teller	Hour	3	$12.00
1.3.7 Teller	Hour	7	$9.00
1.3.8 Receptionist	Hour	3	$8.00
1.4 Accounting			
1.4.1 Chief Financial Officer	Hour	1	$72.00
1.4.2 Vice President	Hour	1	$30.00
1.4.3 Supervisor	Hour	1	$19.00
1.4.4 Clerk	Hour	5	$11.00
1.5 Marketing			
1.5.1 Senior Vice President	Hour	1	$45.00
1.5.2 Coordinator	Hour	1	$19.00
1.5.3 Assistant Coordinator	Hour	1	$16.00
1.5.4 Administrative Assistant	Hour	1	$12.00
1.6 Facilities/Supply			
1.6.1 Supervisor	Hour	1	$26.00
1.6.2 Assistant Supervisor	Hour	1	$22.00

*costs include overhead

		Units of Measure	Quantity Available for Br. Adm. Project	Cost/ Price ($)
	1.6.3 Custodian	Hour	5	$14.00
	1.6.4 Controller	Hour	1	$14.00
	1.6.5 Courier	Hour	1	$12.00
	1.6.6 Administrative Assistant	Hour	1	$10.00
1.7	Human Resources			
	1.7.1 Vice President	Hour	1	$38.00
	1.7.2 Supervisor	Hour	1	$19.00
	1.7.3 Clerk	Hour	3	$15.00
1.8	Legal			
	1.8.1 Senior Vice President	Hour	1	$54.00
	1.8.2 Administrative Assistant	Hour	2	$21.00
1.9	Audit/Compliance			
	1.9.1 Vice President	Hour	2	$27.00
	1.9.2 Clerk	Hour	3	$13.00
1.10	Operations			
	1.10.1 Assistant Vice President	Hour	1	$22.00
	1.10.2 Supervisor	Hour	2	$14.00
	1.10.3 Clerk	Hour	15	$8.00
1.11	MIS			
	1.11.1 Senior Vice President	Hour	1	$45.00
	1.11.2 Assistant Vice President	Hour	2	$21.00
	1.11.3 Supervisor	Hour	1	$17.00
	1.11.4 Clerk	Hour	6	$15.00
2.0 Tools and Machinery				
2.1	Computer			
	2.1.1 Dell P4 2Ghz Workstation	Each	10	$1,230.00
	2.1.2 Dell PowerEdge 1500 Network Server	Each	1	$3,400.00
	2.1.3 Dell PowerEdge 2550 Internet Server	Each	1	$4,150.00
	2.1.4 3Com Hub	Each	5	$1,510.00
	2.1.5 HP ScanJet 4400C	Each	2	$160.00
	2.1.6 HP DeskJet 890C Printer	Each	10	$240.00
	2.1.7 HP 5Si Laser Printer	Each	1	$3,100.00
	2.1.8 HP Color LaserJet 5500 Printer	Each	1	$5,800.00
	2.1.9 3Com Digital Projector	Each	1	$2,800.00
2.2	Office			
	2.2.1 Executone Phone	Each	5	$150.00
	2.2.2 Quart Portable Presentation Screen	Each	1	$170.00

	Units of Measure	Quantity Available for Br. Adm. Project	Cost/ Price ($)
2.2.3 Konica 7050 Copier	Each	1	$4,300.00
2.2.4 Brother IntelliFax Facsimile Machine	Each	3	$350.00
3.0 Installed Equipment and Materials			
3.1 Executive Desk	Each	5	$530.00
3.2 Swivel Adjustable Chair	Each	15	$150.00
3.3 Small Conference Table	Each	3	$225.00
3.4 Metal Secure File Cabinet	Each	8	$125.00
3.5 Portable Office Cubicle	Each	5	$580.00
4.0 Fees, Licenses			
4.1 Microsoft Project 98 Group Discount License	Each	1	$350.00
4.2 Microsoft Office 2000 Suite Group Discount License	Each	1	$625.00
4.3 Adobe Acrobat 5.0 Individual User License	Each	1	$125.00
5.0 Outside Resources			
5.1 Consultant	Hour	5	$85.00
5.2 Junior Consultant	Hour	10	$60.00

Industrial Construction Project

Hierarchical Resource Breakdown Structure

Resources	Unit	Rate	Comments
R-1.0 Personnel			
R-1.1 Staff			All staff fully burdened, includes overhead
R-1.1.1 Project Manager	Hr	S65	
R-1.1.2 Engineer	Hr	S52	
R-1.1.3 Surveyor	Hr	S52	Includes transet and reflectors
R-1.1.4 Scheduler	Hr	S45	
R-1.1.5 Purchaser	Hr	S45	
R-1.1.6 Estimator	Hr	S45	
R-1.1.7 Draftsman	Hr	S36	Includes lofting and shop drawings
R-1.1.8 Traceability Clerk	Hr	$18	Also forklift operator to manage material flow
R-1.2C			
R-1.2.1 Superintendent	Hr	S55	
R-1.2.2 Welder	Hr	S42	Includes welding unit
R-1.2.3 Pipe Mill Operator	Hr	S42	Pipe mill operations in burdened rates
R-1.2.4 Filter	Hr	S40	Includes cutting equipment
R-1.2.5 Rigger	Hr	S3R	
R-1.2.6 Painter	Hr	S30	Performs blasting and painting
R-1.2.7 Scaffoider	Hr	S28	
R-2.0 Equipment			
R-2.1 Crane	Hr	$100	Includes operator in hourly rate
R-2.2 Cherry Picker	Hr	$10	Operated by craft personnel
R-2.3 Grader	Hr	S75	Includes operator in hourly rate
R-2.4 Generator	Hr	$25	Power source for welding units, lights
R-2.5 Compressor	Hr	S25	Supports gouging, painting, pneumatic tools
R-2.6 Man-Lift	Hr	$10	Operated by craft personnel
R-2.7 Scaffolding	Hr	S25	Includes all materials and tools
R-2.8 Gang Boxes			
R-2.8.1 Welding		$10	Includes all handtools and equipment
R-2.8.2 Rigging	Hr	S10	Includes all handtools and equipment
R-2.8.3 Scaffolding	Hr	$10	Includes all handtools and equipment
R-2.8.4 Painting	Hr	$10	Includes all handtools and equipment

Resources	Unit	Rate	Comments
R-3.0 Materials			
R-3.1 Structural			Material costs only
R-3.1.1 Plate	Ton	S650	Piate roiled into various sized tubulars
R-3.1.2 Tubular-18"x.500	LnFt	$60	Vertical bracings
R-3.1.3 Tubular-18"x.375	LnFt	$50	Horizontal bracings
R-3.1.4 Tubular-6"x.375	LnFt	S18	Deck framing
R-3.1.5 Tubular-4"x.375	LnFt	S12	Seafastenings
R-3.1.6 Grating	SqFt	$4	Includes attachment clips
R-3.2 Anodes	Ea	$1,200	Includes delivery to fabrication site
R-3.3 Paint	Gal	$25	Includes all primers and topcoats
R-3.4 Handrails	L.N rt	$75	Includes shop fabrication labor and materials

4 Estimating Models

The most accurate and reliable estimate for a project can be developed when all of the elements of the WBS have been identified with a reasonable degree of reliability and when the RBS has been defined with the desired degree of certainty. This estimate is referred to as the bottom-up estimate, and it is derived from detailed information that is contained in the WBS and RBS at the time of the estimate.

Detailed and accurate estimates require substantial definitive information about the project. They also require a relatively large amount of time and effort for estimating. Therefore, a balance should be struck between the time spent on estimating, the accuracy of the results, and the degree of accuracy required by the stakeholders at the point in the project life.

EARLY ESTIMATES

A project needs estimates for cost and duration even when there is very little information about the project, so that it can be authorized for implementation. Unfortunately, the amount of detail required for a detailed estimate will not be available until a major portion of the project has been designed and implemented. The WBS elements, the resource costs, or the assignment pattern for the various WBS elements might not have been defined. Notwithstanding, the project stakeholders must have indications of the cost and duration of the project to approve it for the earliest stages of implementation. Therefore, an abbreviated version of the WBS and RBS must be developed during the inception stages of the project to formulate a rough estimate of cost and duration for preliminary decision purposes.

As the information in these structures is enhanced, and as each of these structures is expanded in line with available project detail, the project estimate will become more reliable. For example, the initial estimate might be conducted with a WBS that is extended only to Level One and with an RBS that is extended only to Level Two. Then, when more information becomes available, the estimate would be with a Level Three WBS and a Level Five RBS. Depending on the organization, the first estimate is sometimes called "conceptual" or "order of magnitude." This first estimate can be developed using any one of several models, although the analogous estimating technique is used most often for conceptual estimates.

Availability of historical data is paramount in developing and using estimating models, and in the general process of estimating. Specifically, earned value calculations of previously executed projects offer reliable data for testing budgeted cost estimates, thereby offering an opportunity for continuous improvement of accuracy and reliability of the cost estimating process.

Historical data will provide a basis for more reliable conceptual estimates during the initiation stages and for more detailed and realistic plans during the detailed planning stages. Historical project data for construction and industrial projects span several decades and a multitude of project types under numerous implementation constraints. Unfortunately, software and system development projects do not enjoy the same luxury because many software and system development projects are regarded as vastly different from those in the historical database.

In addition to the historical data, the project manager's experience in formulating estimates will contribute to the quality of the estimates for the project. Seasoned project managers often are able to develop estimates that are somewhat realistic because they address all of the important aspects of the deliverables. This elusive experience factor that can allow the project manager to improve the accuracy of an early estimate of the cost and duration of the project, even if they are developed using inexact methods. The experience of the project manager will continue to be a factor in the project's success as it moves into the implementation stages and as the project team must focus on the challenges of optimizing the inevitable changes in cost, schedule, and scope.

During the project's inception phase, very little project-specific information is available, and therefore the estimate is not very accurate (see Figure 4-1). Part of the reason for this inaccuracy is that the probability of undesirable events occurring is very high during the early stages of the project (see Figure 4-2). However, the consequences and associated costs of modifying project objectives are not significant during the early project stages because the effort spent up to that point on the design and implementation of the project is very small (see Figures 4-3 and 4-4).

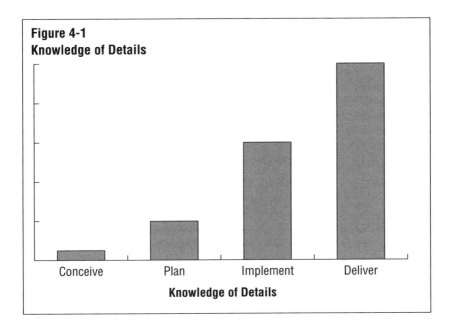

Figure 4-1
Knowledge of Details

Conceive   Plan   Implement   Deliver
Knowledge of Details

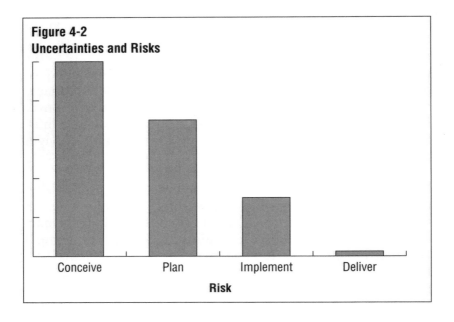

Figure 4-2
Uncertainties and Risks

Conceive   Plan   Implement   Deliver

Risk

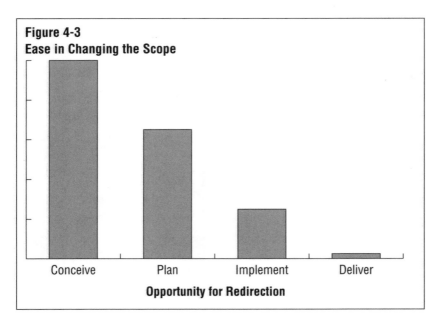

Figure 4-3
Ease in Changing the Scope

Conceive   Plan   Implement   Deliver

Opportunity for Redirection

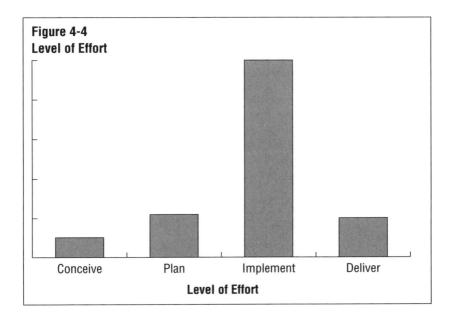

Figure 4-4
Level of Effort

Conceive   Plan   Implement   Deliver

Level of Effort

It would be ideal, although neither realistic nor likely, if all of the project information were available at the time the early estimates are made and if no changes were made to the scope beyond this point in the project. Given that the likelihood of changes occurring in the project scope and project environment at later stages of the project life is almost certain, making midstream changes to the project direction will have significant financial consequences. Sometimes, it is the effects of these scope clarifications or changes that make the original estimate seem highly inaccurate.

It is against this backdrop, and being painfully sensitive to the real possibility of myriad changes during the implementation phase of the project, that the project manager must develop rough estimates for the project during its formative stages. The refinements of the cost and duration estimates are based on more detailed information about the project and are made in the context of new or modified client requirements.

Generally speaking, the changes to the project plans are the results of changes in client requirements, project environment, and technology of the project content, as well as errors. Errors can be divided into errors in design, errors in estimates and schedules, and errors in implementation.

Early estimates, by their very nature, are based on sketchy data and will not have a high degree of accuracy. By comparison, estimates performed late in the development cycle are based on a much wider set of information and thus are very accurate. In other words, early estimates are inaccurate and difficult to make, yet they become the basis for project comparison and for developing guidelines for the final project funding.

When the project is in its inception phases, only a small amount of information is available about the specifics of the project, and yet an estimate is needed to make a decision on the viability of the project and the profitability of the resulting product. It bears repeating that, even though an estimate is needed at that time, those who use the estimate must be made aware of its inaccuracies.

Some organizations hold the project managers to the early estimates of the project. Enlightened organizations allow systematic and logical changes to the project budget throughout the project life cycle.

Given that the project manager will make the estimate as accurate as possible considering the data available, the project stakeholders should keep the limitations of early estimates in mind when selecting projects based on them and during the cost management process, particularly if the project is selected for implementation based on the early estimates. Nonetheless, a preliminary estimate is needed for making project decisions, even though it will have to be made before project objectives are clarified, project scope is defined, requirements are fully spelled out, functions are clearly defined, and project constraints have been fully formulated.

During the early stages of the project, and in the absence of extensive and detailed information about it, project managers use a variety of tools and techniques in formulating the project estimate. These usually are based on models that have proven to be successful during previous estimating efforts, in this project or in others. These models use mathematical expressions, from the very simple to the very complex, or a multitude of assumptions to estimate the cost, duration, and resource demands of a single activity, an assembly, or the entire project as a function of one or more input variables.

The techniques project managers use to make preliminary project estimates include analogous, parametric, modular, ratio, and range estimating. The selection of the technique depends on organizational policies, the project manager's experience, and the amount of information available to the project manager at the time of the estimate.

Normally, estimate models are very easy to use, and they provide a quick prediction of the cost of the project, although the accuracy is not very high, particularly if the model is based on generic historical data rather than on discipline-specific historical data. Therefore, any amount of effort that is spent on customizing the model to a specific project environment within an industry will have significant rewards in terms of increased accuracy and reliability.

Again, the success of the development and use of estimating models is highly dependent upon the experience and competency of project managers and project team members, as well as reliable historical information. Equally important, the enterprise environment should give the project managers applicable incentives to conduct such continuous improvements.

Models used for software and systems development projects use some or all of the following data in arriving at the rough estimate of the project:

- System complexity

- System size

- Manpower skill

- Resource availability

- Specificity of project objectives

- Clarity of requirements

- Operating system features

- Environmental characteristics

- Extent of new technologies involved in the project.

Likewise, models used for construction and industrial projects use the following data in the process of predicting the project cost and duration:

- Industry and project type

- Capacity and quantity

- External and usable size

- Overall weight

- Project location

- Extent to which novel materials, tools, and techniques are required for the project.

Formalizing when, how often, and how estimates of cost and duration should be performed depends on the type of project, the prevailing organizational procedures, and the degree to which the organization is concerned with project cost and any overruns. Ideally, intermediate cost and duration estimates should be performed several times during the project life, and not necessarily at budget authorization milestones. Frequently enhancing the estimate, through regular reviews of all of the cost components, will improve the accuracy of the estimate. It also will provide substantial historical data for refining and enhancing the estimating models of future projects.

Using the earned value method provides an opportunity to test earlier cost estimates of the current project and improve the accuracy of initial and intermediate cost estimates of future projects. With the advent of powerful software and the use of a detailed RBS-WBS in tandem, the estimate update process will become automatic and almost continuous.

BOTTOM-UP ESTIMATING

With a detailed WBS and RBS, a project manager can make a systematic and accurate estimate of the project's required resources—and, therefore, its cost. Once deliverable-oriented WBS elements have been developed for a project, producing a detailed cost estimate becomes a simple matter of mapping the WBS onto the RBS and assigning the appropriate resources to individual WBS elements.

This methodical approach may initially require some extra effort; but if an organization regularly produces and maintains its RBS families, the process becomes remarkably straightforward. Thus, the project manager's anxiety about cost estimating will decrease, and the organization will achieve significant efficiencies in planning, scheduling, and monitoring.

Here the WBS and the RBS work together: Mapping a project's WBS onto the RBS links project activities with specific available resources. After mapping the WBS onto the RBS (represented schematically in Figure 4-5), the money necessary for the project can be estimated by adding the products of the resource quantities demanded by the WBS and the corresponding RBS unit costs. That is, for each element at the lowest level

Figure 4-5
Elemental Estimate

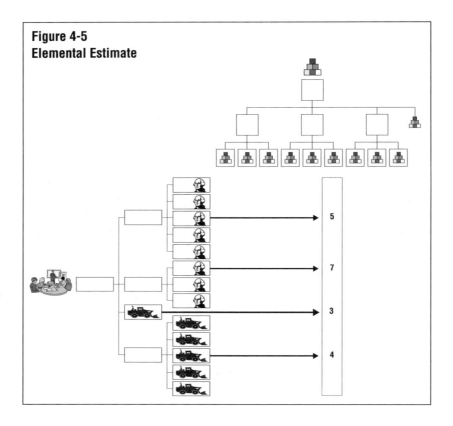

of the WBS, multiply the desired quantity of the resource by its cost per unit of appropriate measure to yield cost. The sum of the cost estimates of all of the WBS elements, individually derived from estimating the resource amounts, is equivalent to the total cost estimate. The resource quantity, known as effort, itself is a product of the resource intensity and duration.

Figure 4-5 captures the essentials of the process of using the WBS and RBS in tandem for developing elemental estimates. Begin at the lowest level of the WBS, which can be denoted as Level N. Calculate the cost of each element by multiplying the quantity of required resources by the unit cost of each resource. The unit cost is obtained from the RBS. The important point here is that the details are not hidden. The category of the resource, its intensity, and its duration are clearly indicated as part of this calculation. For example, if a project needs three brick layers for four days to build a wall, then the category is brick layer, the intensity is three workers, the duration is four days, and the effort is 12 worker days. At a unit cost of $300 per worker per day, the cost is $3,600.

Using the above elemental estimate, the total cost of the project can be found by adding all these costs together. So many numbers are somewhat unwieldy, however, and such a direct calculation of going directly to the top of the WBS might hide some additional useful information that can be obtained easily. Therefore, in the next step, move up a level to determine—now by simple addition—the total quantity of resources necessary for all elements at level N-1, grouped by resource category. Repeat the process, proceeding from bottom to top, until each element of the WBS shows the total resources it requires, grouped by category. In addition to the cost, we now have the resource utilization values for all sub-units defined in the WBS.

Once the calculations are extended to Level Zero, the project's total resource utilization and cost have been determined, as have the total resource utilization and the cost of all intermediate elements of the WBS. As in any method of estimating, the calculated project estimate must be checked against experiential data and the subjective knowledge of project management professionals familiar with this type of project.

Once the first estimate has been developed, the project manager must verify that the estimate for the total cost of the project is reasonable. Since poor overall estimates often result from inadvertent omissions of key elements in the WBS and the RBS, enhancement of the project plan primarily involves filling the logical gaps in the WBS by modifying, deleting, or adding to the current WBS elements.

Correction also may include improving elemental estimates at the lowest levels, but an elemental estimate should not be changed arbitrarily from what one believes is the best estimate. Further, the estimate values for those items that are above Level N should not be changed, as these items can be regarded as the parents of lower-level items. The reason for this exclusion is that all parents' estimates are derived from sums of lower-level estimates and not from direct input.

Project planning documents, including the estimate, should be treated as living documents. As new information becomes available, the WBS, RBS, elemental estimates, and schedule network logic must be updated and refined. In turn, these changes will trigger changes in the overall cost duration of the project. Ideally, these enhancements should be conducted frequently rather than only for specific administrative milestones and budget deadlines. In other words, at every update opportunity, the enhanced WBS (and if necessary, an enhanced RBS) should be used to refine the elemental estimates.

A well-defined, accurate, consistent, and regularly updated WBS and RBS will significantly improve the likelihood that the project will be successful, by facilitating clear plans and good communication. Using a good WBS with an accurate RBS, one can ask detailed cost and resource questions about the project, such as:

- What is the total number of worker hours needed for module A?

- How many worker hours of chemists do we need for modules A, B, and C?

When these elemental and total estimates are combined with a good schedule, questions can then be asked that involve detailed time and resource issues together, such as:

- How many programmers do we need across the entire project in July?

- How many engineers do we need for module C during July?

- Would the demand for client-side programmers be reduced next July if we postpone module B by three months?

- How many more analysts would we need next February if the scope of module D were doubled?

- How would doubling the scope of module G affect project cost, schedule, and resource requirements?

- If Module F were to be delayed six months, what would the resulting cost and schedule look like?

It is highly advisable to develop an optimum project plan—that is, a plan that is unencumbered with milestone constraints and low resource availability and, therefore, is poised to deliver the project in the most efficient and cost-effective manner. This plan should then be considered the pristine project plan. Then, the schedule could be altered to meet client requirements in resources or milestones, with possible impact on project cost. To sum up, rather than starting with a constrained project plan and using it as a baseline, a pristine plan should be the base of comparisons for all plan changes.

ACCURACY

Depending on the time the estimate is prepared and on the volume and quality of historical data available to the project manager at that time, the spectrum of estimates ranges from the very rough to the very detailed. An estimate can be viewed as simply a prediction of the final values of project cost and duration once the project is fully implemented. Thus, the expression of accuracy of the estimate is somewhat akin to the expression of the probability that the actual cost of the project will match this prediction (Anonymous[2] 1999; Vigder and Kark 1994). As noted, this probability, or accuracy, is very low during the early stages of the project and relatively high during the later stages.

Experience in construction and industrial projects has shown that, due to monitoring and reporting inaccuracies, even the estimates that are prepared late in project life are not expected to be more accurate than 3–4 percent. As a general rule, if all the project information is available, which usually occurs in the later stages of the project, the accuracy of the estimate is probably around 3 percent. Therefore, the actual value may be 97–103 percent of the estimate. At the other end of the spectrum, if very little information is available, the accuracy may degrade to 233 percent. In other words, the actual value of the cost of the project might be 33–333 percent of the estimate. Looking at some completed projects, in construction and system development, the cost overrun has been even more than 233 percent. Notwithstanding, estimates developed during the inception process, and in the absence of much project-specific historical information, generally are accurate to an order of magnitude, i.e., the final cost will range from 30 percent to 330 percent of the initial conceptual estimate.

If sufficient project-specific historical data are available to a project manager with ample experience in this area, then that project manager will be able to determine the realistic accuracy of the conceptual estimate, regardless of whether the accuracy is better or worse than an order of magnitude. The key is that if the project manager is more experienced, and more informed, about the current project or about previous similar projects, the estimate will be more useful to the stakeholders because it is more accurate.

For purposes of convenience and standardization in communication, organizations assign specific names for estimates at discrete points in the project life cycle. Such naming convention exists because many organizations require estimate updates only at a few points during the life cycle. Figure 4-6 shows the most common categorization of estimates for external and internal projects. The important thing to remember is that not all organizations use all of these titles. Some organizations may use a subset to identify the estimates prepared for their projects. Some organizations may also use titles that are not on this list.

Figure 4-6
Cost Estimate Titles

- Conceptual
- Order of magnitude
- Feasibility
- Preliminary
- Final
- Definitive
- Capital cost
- Appropriation

It is safe to assign degrees of accuracy to each of these names in internal communications, but it is fair to say that not all organizations attribute the same characteristics and accuracies to a specific estimate label. For example, organizational procedures might specify that if an estimate is labeled as preliminary, then it will be expected to have an accuracy of 30 percent. Regardless of what it is called, the accuracy of the estimate is determined by the nature and accuracy of the historical data, the estimating technique that the project manager has used in formulating it, and the competence of the project manager preparing it.

For purposes of consistency and for communicating across wider administrative boundaries, sometimes organizations adopt titles that are recommended by professional societies such as the Association for the Advancement of Cost Engineering and the Project Management Institute. These professional societies prescribe that, as a general rule, the accuracy of the first formalized and published estimate should be better than –40 percent and +100 percent. For example, the estimator should be reasonably certain that the final actual cost of a project that is initially estimated at $100 should be between $60 and $200.

As the project progresses through its life-cycle stages, and as the detailed project objectives and the data necessary for the estimate become available, more accurate estimates become possible. To use the WBS as a base of reference, when very little information is available about a project, only Level Zero of the WBS, which is the total project, can be estimated using any one of the models described here. Once more information becomes available, individual Level One elements can be estimated, again using these models. The estimate for the project will then be the summary of Level One elements and a more accurate estimate.

Again, as more information becomes available, Level Two items of the WBS will be defined and estimated. Finally, once the project has been divided into its smallest units and planned at the lowest level of the WBS, the lowest-level units will be estimated using experience or appropriate models (see Figure 4-7). Then, these estimates are rolled up to Level One items and to the total project estimate to determine the cost and duration of the project.

The estimate of the total project will be reasonably accurate primarily because all of the elements have been accounted for and estimated. Likewise, the more detailed logic network and the more accurate elemental duration estimate will yield a more reliable project duration.

Alternately, one might consider an array of estimating models, each targeted for a specific point in the project life cycle. During the early stages of the project, when only total-project estimates are sufficient, one would use analogous estimating techniques. Then, once the project gets fleshed out a bit, perhaps to Level Two, parametric estimating models and tools would be used. When the project has been expanded to Levels Three and Four, a bottom-up estimating structure would be established. In turn, this bottom-up estimating structure would be the platform for continuous enhancements to the WBS, RBS, and estimate (see Figure 4-7).

Although simple estimating models are not very accurate estimating tools for the total project if applied only at Level Zero, these models are frequently used, implicitly or explicitly, for estimating lowest-level elements of a project even during its

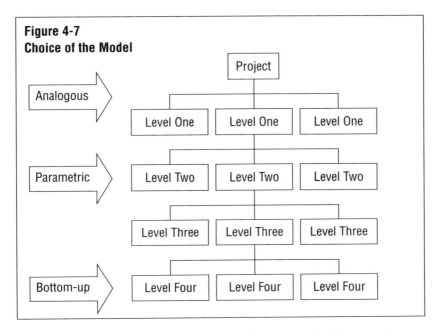

Figure 4-7
Choice of the Model

advanced stages. If no calculation biases are built into the estimating structure, and if the WBS has a large number of lowest-level elements, the repetition and the rollup process will balance the inaccuracies of the models by which the estimates of the lower level elements were prepared.

Estimating models compute the values of a set of dependent outputs, such as cost, duration, or resource utilization, as a function of the values of a set of independent inputs. The timing of the estimate affects how much information is available and how reliable it is. Very early estimates are based on sparse and incomplete data regarding the project and the development process, and thus are not very accurate.

PARAMETRIC ESTIMATING

The terms "parametric estimating" and "modular estimating" refer to two estimating models that have been used in different industries and therefore have taken on different names. These two models are essentially very similar in usage, principle, and underlying structure. After describing their similarities and differences, we will use the term "parametric estimating" to refer to both of these techniques collectively.

Modular estimating is normally used for projects that have physical deliverables, such as refineries, power stations, office buildings, or manufacturing plants. Using this approach, the facility is characterized by indices describing the quantity and size of several key components, such as power rating and number of pumps, physical size of pumps and turbines, size of the plant floor, capacity and number of cranes, etc. The modular model then uses historical data and predictive formulas that have been developed for the characteristics of the modules to develop estimates for the project's cost, duration, and the amount of resources necessary. Modular estimating is used primarily in construction, process, and manufacturing projects (Figure 4-8).

Similar to the modular model, the parametric model uses historical data as the basis of its predictive features. However, the characteristics that will become the input into the process are based primarily on performance indicators such as speed, accuracy, tolerance, reliability, user-friendliness, error rate, and complexity of the environment of the deliverables. Parametric estimating is used primarily in software development and system development projects. The output of parametric models includes the cost and duration of major phases, total project cost, and resource requirements.

Figure 4-8
Modular and Parametric Models

- Physical characteristics
  - Flow capacity
  - Storage capacity
  - Number of equipment
  - Size of equipment

- Performance attributes
  - Speed
  - Accuracy
  - Error tolerance
  - Reliability
  - User-friendliness

Generally speaking, parametric/modular models calculate the dependent variables of cost and duration on the basis of one or more independent variables. These independent variables are quantitative indices of performance or physical attributes. More sophisticated models can provide a multitude of levels of estimates depending on the input information available. If, during the early stages of the project, a small array of data regarding the project is available, a rough cost estimate is provided for the project. However, if a large array of project data becomes available later in the project's life cycle, more accurate estimates containing estimates of resources and duration will be calculated using the same model.

A parametric model for a construction or process project would use the data provided by the user on any or all of the following characteristics: project type, frame material, exterior material, ground conditions, desired floor space, and roof type. Then, using the general relationships developed between these input variables and the output variables, the model would provide an estimate of some or all of the output variables. The output variables include cost of the design process, cost of the structure, size of major equipment, optimum size of the construction crew, size of the parking lot, duration of the structure construction and equipment installation, and overall project duration (see Figure 4-9).

Figure 4-9
Construction and Industrial Projects

- Input
  - Project type
  - Frame material
  - Exterior material
  - Roof type
  - Ground conditions
  - Desired floor space
  - Equipment type

- Output
  - Design cost
  - Structure cost
  - Equipment cost
  - Crew size
  - Labor cost
  - Phase duration
  - Project duration

Input variables for a parametric estimate for a software development project include desired reliability, database size, complexity of technology, size of the deliverable, lines of code, pages of website, number of database records, queries per second, maximum error rate, and function points. The function points index is determined from a weighted summation of user requirements in the areas of inputs, outputs, logic files, inquiries, and interfaces. Other inputs include indicators of project environment and quantified or semi-specific project team characteristics, such as skill level, physical location, and administrative affiliation.

Output variables include resources needed for requirement analysis, system design, system coding, testing, integration, documentation, and system transition. Sometimes the output values include cost and duration of project elements and, by extension, those of the entire project (see Figure 4-10).

Many organizations have developed proprietary parametric models for projects in their own specialty. Depending on the organizational environment and the nature of targeted projects, these models use different statistically derived algorithms—which in turn would use different sets of input and output data—in calculating the output variables based on the input variables. Normally, parametric estimate models are refined and fine-tuned for specific projects within specific industries. These models are, or should be, regularly evalu-

---

Figure 4-10
Systems Development Projects

- Input
  - Reliability
  - Database size
  - Project complexity
  - Error rate
  - Number of queries
  - Function points
  - Labor skills

- Output
  - Analysis cost
  - Implementation cost
  - Transition cost
  - Testing cost
  - Labor cost
  - Phase duration
  - Project duration

ated, validated, calibrated, and customized for accuracy and appropriateness.

Given that the time frame for using the parametric model is the same as that for project selection and project initiation, the estimates of cost and duration developed by the parametric model are usually used for establishing a preliminary budget for the project. In turn, this preliminary budget will be used to compare its financial desirability with the enterprise's other projects.

The utility of parametric estimates will be dramatic if the process is used to develop several estimates for alternate configurations of the same potential project. However, it would be extremely dangerous to use the results of a parametric model to develop definitive budgets, unless the organization is so enlightened that it allows major budget modifications as the estimate matures throughout the life of the project.

ANALOGOUS ESTIMATING

Analogous techniques are among the simplest forms of estimating. In this process, the project manager believes there is significant similarity between the proposed project and projects in the historical database. Analogous models tend to be less complex, easier to use, and more inexact than parametric models. They normally are used for early estimates that are called order of magnitude, conceptual, or ballpark estimates. These early estimates are used to formulate rough estimates for various options and to determine the relative viability of a given project in the process of screening alternative projects.

Given that the purpose of analogous models is to develop order of magnitude estimates based on scarce information, the project manager might be forced to make several assumptions about some of the project's environmental or functional characteristics, such as design attributes, systems engineering process, implementation techniques, and resource availability. It would be helpful to document the assumptions together with the estimate to refine the estimating process for future projects.

When developing the analogous estimate, the project manager should locate and use the values of as many of the following deliverable indices as available: type, functions, requirements, design characteristics, capacity, size, location, cost constraints, and quality expectations. Here again, the project manager's experience will be the deciding factor in judging the proposed project to be similar to those in the database that have formed the basis for developing and customizing the model.

Since the analogous estimating technique is based on actual experience, some software development project managers contend that such estimating has limited use in that industry because, in many instances, no truly similar projects exist in the historical database and that software and system development projects have no true historical precedents. These concerns should subside as more informed project managers collect and refine historical project data on software project languages, development methodologies, resource utilization, and complexity of system development projects—together with cost and schedule history, of course.

The analogous estimate tools described here are ratio estimating, range estimating, the three-quarters rule, the square-root rule, and the two-thirds rule. The significance of the structure of these models is that they were devised before the days of PCs, and thus they contain relatively simple, but powerful, processes for making manual computations more straightforward.

In the absence of extensive historical data for a specific project, these basic models can provide a good first approximation for the estimate of project cost and duration. If these models are customized for each industry sector, the accuracy and reliability of the results will be substantially higher. Therefore, the project manager should keep detailed records of the performance of ongoing projects in order to provide further data for that specific model. Such performance data can conveniently be used to develop refined exponents or ratios for use in estimating the forthcoming projects. The refinement can be focused on a specific industry or even a specific organization within that industry.

Until the full complement of project details for individual elements of the WBS becomes available, the project manager will provide an analogous estimate of the total project based on minimal project-specific information. With expanded information about the project, the project manager develops analogous estimates of the items at the lower levels of the WBS, for example, Levels One and Two. Then, as additional information becomes available, lower level items are estimated. Thus, estimates of project cost and duration gradually become more accurate, complete, and definitive.

The key is that by using a WBS as the base of reference, two subsequent estimates are not new estimates; they simply are enhancements of the original estimate. Therefore, any variances between two successive estimates can be explained and defended more logically and rationally.

Ratio Estimating

This estimating technique is interchangeably called equipment ratio or capacity factor. It is one of the more frequently used forms of estimating in construction, industrial, and process projects. Its premise is that there is a linear relationship among the cost and duration of the project and one or more of the basic features of the proposed project. The basic deliverable features to be quantified and used in this process can be related to either physical attributes or performance characteristics. The so-called ratios or factors are refined from personal experience, company files, or published industry-specific data. Although ratio estimating is deceptively simple, given an extensive array of historical data, it can be a very powerful tool in developing quick estimates for prospective projects.

Examples of ratio estimating include:

- Experience has shown that the cost of major turbines and generators in a power generation plant is nearly 30 percent of the total cost of the plant.

- In a construction project, the total cost of the project is twice that of the materials and embedded equipment.

- The cost of the high-level design of a systems development project is nearly 30 percent of the total cost of the project.

- Only 20 percent of the cost and effort of a systems project is spent in coding.

- Seventy-five percent of the cost of a systems development project is for labor.

- The cost of the engineering design of a facility is nearly 8 percent of the total budget of the project.

(Anonymous[2] 1999; Anonymous[4] 2000; Anonymous[5] 1999; Vigder and Kark 1994.)

Further, there have been extensive efforts in developing a relationship between the estimated lines of code and the total cost of a systems development project, although this ratio is highly specific to the operating system and system architecture.

Range Estimating

Another approach to increasing the reliability of early estimates is to define the range of possible values for the cost of a specific element. The advantage of this technique is that the estimator embeds the accuracy of the estimate in the estimate itself. Thus, an upper limit and lower limit are cited for each of the Level One elements of the project, and the summation of these limits provides an upper and lower limit for the cost of the total project. Similarly, these two limits, combined with a network logic diagram, can provide two different predictions for the delivery duration: shortest and longest. Obviously, as more information about the project becomes available, the range between the highest and lowest numbers of cost and duration will narrow.

A more sophisticated form of this technique is called triple point estimating, in which three separate numbers are cited for cost and duration: most optimistic, most likely, and most pessimistic. This concept was the foundation of the PERT technique, by which probabilistic project duration is obtained by using multiple durations defined for individual activity durations. Then, in addition to the deterministic project duration defined by the estimator's prediction, a range of probable and likely duration values is computed.

Range estimating uses the same statistical fundamentals in estimating total project cost based on probabilistic elemental costs. Thus, in addition to providing one number as the total possible cost of an element of the WBS, which reflects the opinion of the project manager, two other values are also provided. One is the most pessimistic estimate and the other is the most optimistic estimate. Using these three values, the calculated most likely cost for the element, or the project, can be determined.

Equally useful, if this three-value set is available for all of the elements of a fully developed WBS, is a Monte Carlo random number generation tool, which can be used to develop a statistically likely cost for the project. This three-number set will allow development of probability distributions for the project cost and a probable cost for the project based on random selection of elemental estimates.

In many cases, the most likely values derived from the application of this statistical method are higher than the deterministic values derived from the summation of single-estimate values

---

Figure 4-11
Range Estimating

- Elements
  −Optimistic time (TO)
  −Most likely time (TM)
  −Pessimistic time (TP)
- Calculate expected time for each activity
  −TE = (TO + 4TM + TP) / 6
  −Standard deviation = (TP −TO) / 6

---

provided by the project manager. This revelation highlights the premise that project managers and project estimators are fundamentally optimistic and hence tend to underestimate the cost and duration of a project. Figure 4-11 shows the calculation of elemental values of most likely costs based on the three values provided by the project manager.

If the three estimate values provided by the project manager are 5, 8, and 35, the most likely estimate for that element, as provided by this model, is 12. The net result of using this model is that the estimate becomes steered toward the mean of the optimistic and pessimistic values, primarily because the deterministic value is dangerously close to the most optimistic value. On the other hand, if the three estimates provided by the project manager are 5, 20, and 35, the most likely value predicted by this model will be 20; note that 20 is the estimate that was considered most likely by the project manager. The point is not that every deterministic estimate should be the mean of optimistic and pessimistic values, but that project managers should not be overly optimistic in estimating every aspect of the project.

Finally, although range estimating is normally used to develop a WBS fully, they are far more valuable when the WBS elements have not been fully defined beyond the first and second levels and when the cost of these elements is at the order-of-magnitude accuracy.

The Three-Quarters Rule

The three-quarters rule provides a simple method of developing the estimate for a proposed project's cost by comparing the capacity of the existing and the proposed deliverable. The capacity index can be the size, speed, complexity, or accuracy of the deliverable in question. The decision as to which index to use for the rough estimate will depend on the project's objectives, on whatever information is available at the time the estimate is made, and finally on the experience of the project manager.

Given that the relationship between any two facets of the project and the total cost may not follow the same pattern, several different size or capacity indices might produce several different estimates for the new project. Averaging the resulting estimates will provide a more accurate estimate. Therefore, for best results, as many indices as possible should be used to determine the estimate—that is, of course, if there are enough historical data to use in developing several ratio relationships in a given project. Then, by simple or weighted averaging of these individual estimates, a more tempered project estimate can be obtained.

This estimating rule is a slightly more sophisticated version of the ratio estimating technique. The ratio technique uses a linear relationship between the equipment size and total cost, whereas the three-quarters rule uses an exponential function in predicting the overall project cost.

The three-quarters rule is based on the formula shown in Figures 4-12 and 4-13. Its premise is that if the ratio of the capacities, or sizes, of the proposed and current projects is raised to the power of three-fourths, it will provide an indicator of the ratio of the cost of the two projects. This technique can be used to make extrapolations or interpolations either graphically or computationally, and both can be performed using spreadsheet software. If the historical database includes data for only one similar project, this technique can be used numerically.

Figure 4-12
Analogous Estimating Rules of Thumb

- Three-Quarters Rule
  $C_p = C_e(S_p/S_e)^{.75}$
- Square-Root Rule
  $T_p = T_e(C_p/C_e)^{.5}$
- Two-Thirds Rule
  $T_p = T_e(N_p/N_e)^{.66}$

Figure 4-13
Analogous Estimating Rules of Thumb (Variables)

T_p, T_e = Project duration
C_p, C_e = Cost
S_p, S_e = Size or capacity
N_p, N_e = Concurrent subsystems

Figure 4-14
Three-Quarters Rule (Estimate Cost of a House Based on the Number of Bedrooms)

Current house: three bedrooms = $375,000
Proposed house: five bedrooms

(Cost of new house)/(375,000) = ((5)/(3))**(3/4)
Cost of a five-bedroom house = $550,070

Cost of a six-bedroom house = $630,670
Cost of a two-bedroom house = $276,670

However, if the database contains data for several similar projects, the graphic technique might be more convenient.

Figure 4-14 shows the computational application of this rule to predict the cost of houses with two, five, or six bedrooms, in which the only cost information that the project manager has is the cost for a three-bedroom house. Figure 4-15 shows a graphic application of the same example. If a log-log scale is

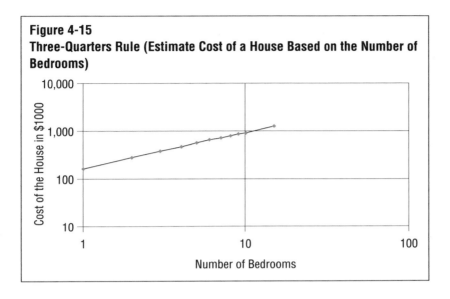

Figure 4-15
Three-Quarters Rule (Estimate Cost of a House Based on the Number of Bedrooms)

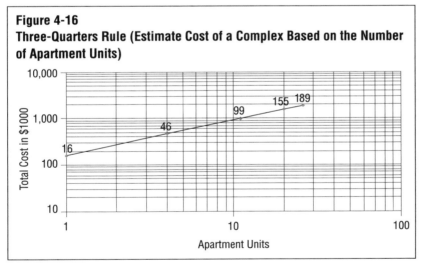

Figure 4-16
Three-Quarters Rule (Estimate Cost of a Complex Based on the Number of Apartment Units)

employed when using the graphic application of this method, the model data will be displayed in a straight line, which would make visual interpolation very easy. Figure 4-16 shows the application of this technique to the cost of apartment complexes based on the number of units in each complex.

If enough industry-specific or organization-specific data are available, this technique can be refined to reflect the specifics of that particular capacity index for projects in that organization. Then, for future estimates, a customized variation of this technique will be used to arrive at more accurate conceptual estimates. This modification can be referred to as the modified three-quarters rule.

Thus, using the existing data, an exponent other than three-fourths will be suggested for this particular project environment. Again, the cost exponent will be different for different capacity indices; therefore, a different exponent must be developed for each capacity index. The resulting estimates can then be combined to formulate a more refined one.

Figure 4-17 shows how an exponent of .96 was obtained for a particular class of construction projects. Computing and recording the value of the exponents are necessary only in the computational method. If you use the graphic method, you need not be aware of the value of the exponent. Thus, using a straight-line extrapolation, or interpolation, you can determine the cost of the proposed project.

Figure 4-18 shows a graphic application of this extrapolation technique without any specific reference to the value of the exponent. Using as few as two data points, the straight line defin-

---

Figure 4-17
Modified Three-Quarters Rule (Estimate Cost of a House Based on the Number of Bedrooms)

Current house: three-bedroom house = $700,000
Current house: four-bedroom house = $900,000

Proposed house: six-bedroom house?

$(900/700) = ((4/3)**?)$ $? = 0.96$

(Cost of new house)/(700,000) = ((6)/(3))**(.96)

Cost of new house = $1,280,000

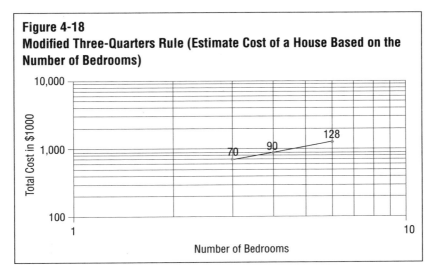

Figure 4-18
Modified Three-Quarters Rule (Estimate Cost of a House Based on the Number of Bedrooms)

ing the model can be defined based on which future estimates can be made very quickly. Figure 4-19 shows the application of this model to estimate the cost of airport expansions (Remer and Wong 1996). This model used the cost of completed airports, such as Newark, JFK, and Hartsfield, to develop a conceptual estimate for the total cost of Denver Airport. The capacity index that was used for comparison was the size of the terminal in square feet.

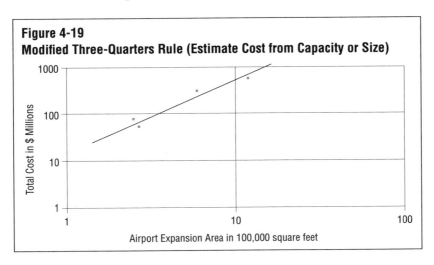

Figure 4-19
Modified Three-Quarters Rule (Estimate Cost from Capacity or Size)

The Square-Root Rule

The square-root technique will allow the project manager to predict the duration of a proposed project on the basis of the costs and durations of the existing project and the cost of the proposed project. The square-root rule is based on the formula that is shown in Figure 4-12. The premise of this rule is that the square root of the ratio of the costs of the proposed and current projects will provide an indicator of the ratio of their duration.

Figures 4-20 and 4-21 show the application of the computational mode of this technique to determine the cost and construction duration of a 340-room dormitory at a time when the only pieces of information available are the cost and duration of the construction of 200-room dormitory. Figure 4-22 shows the graphic representation of a model developed from historical highway construction data.

With existing data from previous similar projects, an industry-specific exponent can be developed. This modification can be referred to as the modified square-root technique. Figures 4-23 and 4-24 show the computational and graphic development of the exponent for process plants on the basis of existing projects. The graphic or the computational method then can be used for future projects. Figure 4-25 shows the graphic application of this technique to the airport expansion data mentioned in the previous section.

Figure 4-20
Square-Root Rule (Dormitory Estimate Duration from Cost)

Current facility: 200 rooms, 12 months, $10.4 million

Proposed facility: 340 rooms, $14.8 million

(Duration for new facility)/(12) = ((14.8)/(10.4))**(1/2)

Duration for new facility = 14.3 months

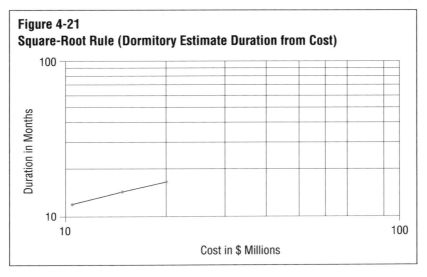

Figure 4-21
Square-Root Rule (Dormitory Estimate Duration from Cost)

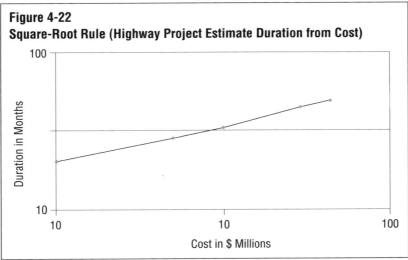

Figure 4-22
Square-Root Rule (Highway Project Estimate Duration from Cost)

The Two-Thirds Rule

The two-thirds technique will allow the project manager to sharpen the estimate of a proposed project's cost or duration if the project contains several concurrent and similar activities. This adjustment is intended to refine the estimates when the

Figure 4-23
Modified Square-Root Rule (Estimate Duration from Cost)

Current facility: 13 months, $20 million
Current facility: 15 months, $25 million

(15/(13) = ((25)/(20)**(?)   ? = 0.641

Proposed facility: $29 million

(Duration of proposed facility)/(15) = (29/25)**.641

Duration of proposed facility = 16.5 months

Figure 4-24
Modified Square-Root Rule (Estimate Duration from Cost)

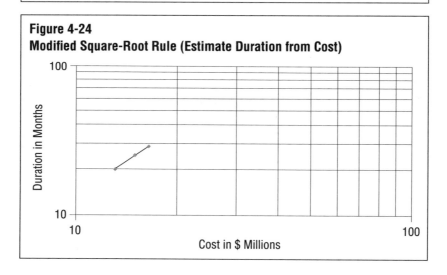

same project personnel are assigned to similar tasks within the project or within a unified program to similar projects.

The two-thirds rule is based on the formula shown in Figure 4-12. Its premise is that raising the ratio of the number of concurrent subsystems to the power of two-thirds will provide an indicator of the ratio of the duration of the two projects. Examples include building several apartment complexes at the same time, designing several web pages at the same time, building several specialty airplanes at the same time, installing

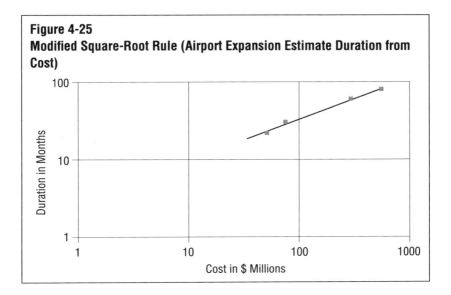

Figure 4-25
Modified Square-Root Rule (Airport Expansion Estimate Duration from Cost)

several servers at the same time, or pulling several sets of fiber-optic cables at the same time.

Although the example using this model addresses only the duration of the project, the presumption is that the multiple concurrent systems will affect the cost of the project in the same manner as they affect the duration. Finally, as in previous models, a sufficient amount of historical data will allow customization of the exponent of this model to specific project environments, maybe with different exponents for cost and duration.

EXPERT JUDGMENT

The expert judgment technique involves consulting one or more experts to validate the estimate of the proposed project against the experience and understanding of the experts, who will consider the details of project complexities and characteristics in tempering the estimate or concurring with it. Many semi-experienced project managers depend on more experienced project managers and experts in the field to validate a project's conceptual estimates, regardless of how the semi-experienced project manager prepared the estimate. Even experienced project managers often consult with their peers to fine-tune what they believe is a reasonable estimate.

Primarily, using an expert judgment opinion is somewhat akin to identifying and using the results of a parametric technique of a personal nature, which is based on intuition, experience, and unarticulated indices. Nonetheless, until such time that these unspoken extrapolations of parametric techniques are formalized, expert judgment will remain one of the more reliable sources of checking the accuracy of the estimates, particularly in software and systems development projects.

NORMALIZATION

If the historical data available to the project managers cover projects completed over several years and many different locations, they must be normalized for time and location before using them in the estimating model. Thus, before the cost and duration of a proposed project can be predicted from historical data, the historical values of cost and duration need to be adjusted and normalized in the light of time and location differences between the proposed project and those that formed the basis for the model (see Figure 4-26).

The term "time" refers to the time span from the year in which the project in the database was completed until today. The inflation rate, or the time value of money, would provide a simple multiplier that can be used to adjust the estimated cost of the proposed project based on the actual costs of existing projects. The term "location adjustment" would account for the differences in salaries and cost of materials in different locations. The comparison between the cost of living at locations of the database projects and that of the proposed project would be another normalization issue.

For example, if the database contains information from projects that have been performed in the United States, and if the

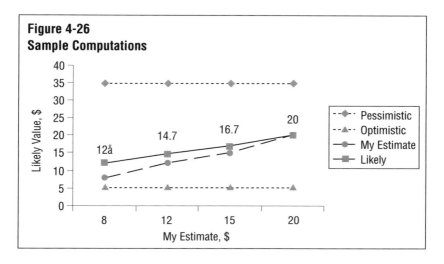

Figure 4-26
Sample Computations

proposed project is to be performed in China or Italy, differences in locality-based cost factors must be considered when finalizing the estimate for project cost. This adjustment is conducted by a simple ratio adjustment. For example, once the time-adjusted estimate of a project is determined, then that estimate will be adjusted again by a factor of, say, 1.12 to account for the project cost difference in those two locations.

Estimating models are the tools that leverage the estimator's experience and the admittedly sparse project data in developing a prediction for the final cost of the project. This leveraging becomes more effective and almost approaches a science when the tool is modified and sharpened with historical data pertaining to the area of the project. Given that early estimates have a profound effect on whether the project gets authorized, estimating models tend to take on a pivotal role in project selection and in developing planning-phase estimates. Conceptually, any estimating model can be used to predict the cost of projects in any industry, although estimating professionals in different industries have gravitated to specific models.

5 Scheduling

The term "schedule" commonly brings to mind the graphical representation of the project activities, including the duration of each activity, the interrelationships among activities, the dates of calculated or imposed milestones, and possibly the completion date of the project. The schedule can be represented graphically in different formats: Gantt charts, milestone charts, or schedule logic networks. These graphical presentations should be based on quantitative data derived from calculations.

Scheduling is not merely the process of assigning calendar dates to the completion of activities of the project, however. It also is the art and science of developing a predicted delivery or completion date for the project by way of developing a logical sequence structure for the project's activities. The foundation of the scheduling process is the logical sequence of the elements of the schedule network, and this sequence serves as the basis for planning, resource allocation, and resource leveling.

The data provided as part of the scheduling process support management decision-making about a project's time, cost, and risk management issues. Although calculations can be performed using the sequence logic depicted in a tabular manner, sometimes using the visual depiction of the network diagram is more convenient for conducting schedule computations. Additionally, some schedulers include many of the results of the scheduling calculations directly on the network diagram.

During the early planning stages, a total overall estimate of project duration can be obtained using any one of the estimating models described in the earlier chapters. However, as more details of the project become available, a more definitive, more logical, and more accurate depiction of the project's duration will become necessary.

A detailed set of WBS and RBS, and the resultant time estimate for each project element, are prerequisites to developing a project schedule (see Figure 5-1). Whereas estimating the cost of higher-level WBS elements is achieved by rolling up the costs of corresponding lower-level elements, estimating the duration of the higher-level WBS elements, and the project, is dependent upon the execution sequence of the lowest WBS elements, as indicated in the logic network. As the details of the project become more accurate, the project's duration and delivery date can be calculated using the network logic diagram (see Figures 5-2 and 5-3).

The logic network is constructed in the context of the interdependency of activities as indicated by work-related constraints. The network diagram will show the sequencing relationship among the project's activities. The estimate of the project's duration will be obtained by calculating the longest chain in the network in light of the sequence of activities and using the estimated activity durations. This chain also represents the shortest duration of the project, given the current logic and the optimum duration of individual elements and activities.

The calendar start date is not required for developing the logic diagram, calculating the floats, or identifying the critical path. However, to assign calendar dates for the start and finish of

---

Figure 5-1
Estimating

- Determine types of resources and their quantities for all WBS items
- Estimate for each WBS item at the lowest level
- Summarize across WBS lines
- Summarize across RBS lines

Figure 5-2
Schedule Activities

- Use WBS listing of activities
- Identify activity details
- Define network interrelationships
  - –At the detail level
  - –At summary levels

Figure 5-3
Scheduling

- Assign a starting date to the project
- Determine the optimum duration for each activity
- Establish the logical sequence for activities
- Conduct a forward pass to determine early dates
- Conduct a backward pass to determine late dates
- Determine floats in the schedule
- Assign the floats

---

activities, and the project as a whole, a calendar start date is necessary.

TWO BASIC NETWORKING TECHNIQUES

There are two basic techniques for developing the schedule network and displaying the relationships among the activities of the network (see Figure 5-4): the Critical Path Method (CPM), also known as the Activity on Arrow Technique (AOA) or the Arrow Diagramming Method (ADM); and the Program Evaluation and Review Technique (PERT), also called the Activity on Node Technique or the Precedence Diagramming Method. These sets of names and their associated acronyms highlight the different features of these techniques.

The CPM, or AOA, technique identifies each activity with two numbers, one signifying the start point and the other signifying the end point (see Figure 5-5). To depict activity relation-

Figure 5-4
Schedule Network Diagramming Methods

- Activity on Node
  −PERT (Project Evaluation and Review Technique)
  −PDM (Precedence Diagramming Method)
- Activity on Arrow
  −CPM (Critical Path Method)
  −ADM (Arrow Diagramming Method)

ships fully, additional relationships among activities must be signified by arrows between activities. These additional relationships are shown using elements that are called dummy activities. Dummy activities are similar to normal activities in notation, except that they are not real activities because there are no resources attached to them, and their duration of execution is zero.

To illustrate, Figure 5-5 shows that Activity F has two predecessors, Activities A and D. To maintain identity and correct linkages, a dummy activity is shown between nodes 2 and 5, which requires no resources and does not consume time. As noted, the AOA notation for network activities contains the relationship information, which makes it easy to store and transfer

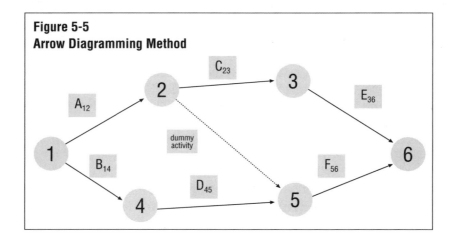

Figure 5-5
Arrow Diagramming Method

network information. Additionally, the logic network can be drawn simply from the list of activities.

The PERT technique, otherwise known as the AON, identifies each activity with one number (see Figure 5-6). On the other hand, another instrument called the Precedence Table would be needed to specify the necessary activity relationships (see Figure 5-7). The other difference between the AOA and AON techniques is that in an AOA network the relationship between

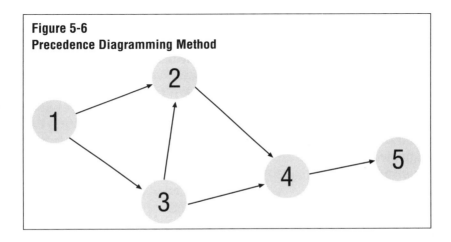

Figure 5-6
Precedence Diagramming Method

Figure 5-7
Precedence Table

Activity	Predecessor
1	---
2	1, 3
3	1
4	2, 3
5	4

two successive activities is usually in the simple finish to start (FS) mode, whereas in a AON network the activity relationships can be signaled by three other relationship notations, namely, start-start (SS), start-finish (SF), and finish-finish (FF).

Notwithstanding the differences, these two techniques have several similarities. Both use forward pass and backward pass to identify the critical path and the amount of floats for non-critical activities. The resulting critical paths will have the same duration and the same floats for the non-critical activities. Further, even though the PERT technique was the first technique to use statistical analysis of the project duration and its associated probability distributions, a CPM network also can benefit from the same set of calculations.

Both of these techniques were used with equal frequency until the mid-eighties. Since then, due to the influence of software tools and other historical issues, the AON technique has gained much more popularity and much wider use. Accordingly, we will use this technique in most of our examples and illustrations.

COMMON CALCULATIONS

Two sets of calculations, forward pass and backward pass, are fundamental to the process of calculating the duration of the project (see Figure 5-8). During the forward pass, go forward from left to right, adding the duration of each activity to the duration of the chain of activities at that point. This set of calculations will take you from the start of the project to its completion in many separate activity chains. The forward pass will identify the shortest duration of project implementation, which is the longest chain within the project, known as the critical path.

Additional information can be obtained from the network data by conducting a backward pass. During the backward pass, go backward from right to left, subtracting the duration

---

Figure 5-8
Schedule Network Diagramming Methods

- Forward Pass
  - –Early start
  - –Early finish
- Backward Pass
  - –Late start
  - –Late finish
- Total Float
- Free Float
  - –Float management guidelines

---

of each activity from the duration of the chain of activities at that point. This set of calculations will take you from the end of the project to its start point in all of the activity chains.

When conducting the forward pass and the backward pass, one of two notations can be used for the addition and subtraction of durations and for the start and finish dates of activities. One is the traditional schema in which the starting point of an activity is 8 a.m. of the start day, and the end point of the activity is 5 p.m. of the finish day. For example, if a sequence of activities includes two activities of three and five days' duration, respectively, the start and finish days of the first activity are 1 and 3, while the start and finish of the second activity occur at day 4 and day 8.

The second calculation schema has been introduced in the past 20 years and is used primarily in the IT industry. It uses 5 p.m. as the start point of one activity and the end point of another activity. Using this notation, the start–finish days of the activities in the example are 0–3 and 3–8.

Schedule calculations of a forward pass and a backward pass depend on good estimates for the durations of the activities and a realistic sequencing logic. The relationship among activities is represented by a precedence table in which the order of execution is highlighted. The precedence table is refined by using a relationship qualifier, which can be FS, FF, or SS.

Figure 5-9 shows the graphic depiction of these relationship qualifiers. Additional helpful information for a good schedule is the appropriate lead and lag times, which should be based on experiential data representing good practices. A lag signifies the number of units of time by which an activity, in an FS relationship, must delay its start after the preceding activity has been completed. Conversely, a lead signifies the number of time units by which a succeeding activity will start before the preceding activity is completed.

Forward pass involves calculating the project duration from project start to finish (left to right), which would help to determine the earliest time when an activity can start (ES) and the earliest time when it can finish (EF). The ES and EF of an activity are determined by adding the duration of an activity to the finish date of the activities preceding it.

Backward pass computation will use the project duration that was calculated as part of the forward pass as the starting point of the computations. Then, the latest time when an activity can start (LS) and the latest time when an activity can finish (LF) can be determined. The LS of an activity will be determined by

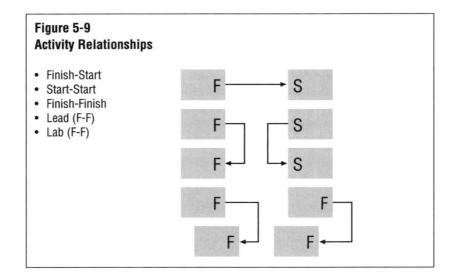

Figure 5-9
Activity Relationships

- Finish-Start
- Start-Start
- Finish-Finish
- Lead (F-F)
- Lab (F-F)

subtracting the duration of an activity from the LS of its succeeding activity.

The significance of ES and EF are that the dates are the earliest dates that the activity in question can start and finish without affecting other activities. Likewise, LS and LF flag the latest date at which activities can start and finish without affecting other activities. By comparing the data from the forward pass and backward pass, namely the values for ES-EF-LS-LF, one can determine the float of an activity, also known as slack. The float can be determined either from LS-ES or LF-EF. (If these two computations result in different floats for the same activity, there is an error in the previous computations.)

The float of an activity is the amount of time that the activity can be delayed without affecting the start date or finish date of other activities. Low values of float, and a small number of activities that have float, will signal the extent to which the project is likely to require complex schedule management policies to remain on target. On the positive side, high amounts of float, and a large number of activities with float, in a network denote flexibility associated with managing the project schedule.

Some of the activities in the network diagram will have identical values of ES and LS, or EF and LF. In other words, these activities will have zero float. The string, or strings, of activities in the network that have zero float is called the critical path of the network (see Figure 5-10).

The critical path determines the total duration of the project, which is the longest chain of the network. It is possible that a

Figure 5-10
Critical Path

- Path(s) with no float
- Path that has the longest duration
- Path duration determines project duration
- Any delay will delay project

project may have more than one critical path but the duration for all critical paths is equal. A delay in any of the activities on the critical path will delay the project completion by the same amount.

Figures 5-11 through 5-15 demonstrate the project network development and schedule calculations. Figure 5-11 shows the activity name, its ID, duration, and precedence list of a network. For simplicity, all the relationships are shown as finish to start (FS), which is the default in network development. Using the duration values and precedence relationships, a network schedule is developed (see Figure 5-12).

After the project network logic is defined with interdependencies, forward pass calculations will calculate the early start and

Figure 5-11
Schedule Calculations (Activity List and Precedence List)

	ID	Duration	Predecessors	Resource Names
A	1	5 days		
B	2	7 days	1	
C	3	3 days	1	
D	4	2 days	3	
E	5	5 days	2, 4, 8, 10	
F	6	8 days	1	
G	7	7 days	6	
H	8	4 days	7	
I	9	3 days	1	
J	10	2 days	9	

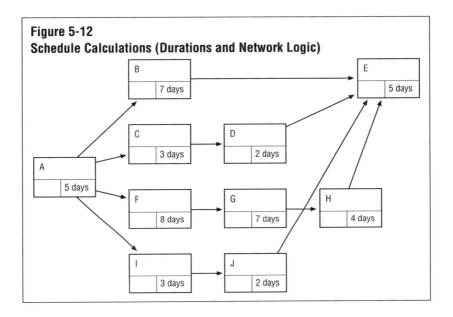

Figure 5-12
Schedule Calculations (Durations and Network Logic)

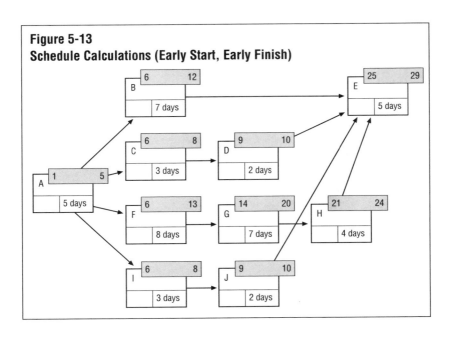

Figure 5-13
Schedule Calculations (Early Start, Early Finish)

Figure 5-14
Schedule Calculations (Late Start, Late Finish)

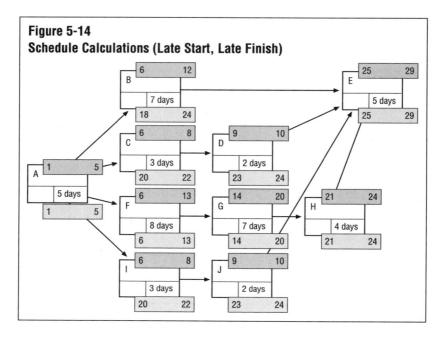

Figure 5-15
Schedule Calculations (Float)

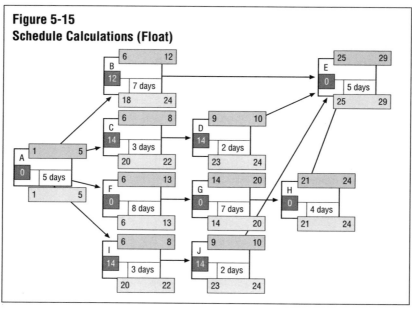

early finish values, which can be added right on the network (see Figure 5-13). Figure 5-14 then shows the results of the backward pass. The key in these passes is that the forward pass is conducted by adding durations, whereas the backward pass is conducted by subtracting durations. Finally, a comparison of the early and late values will determine the amount of float (total float) for these activities.

There are two different categories of float: total float and free float. The amount of float that is calculated from the subtraction of, for example, LS-ES, will signify the total float of that activity. In most cases, the free float is the same as the total float. However, if the network contains a stand-alone chain of several activities, they would end up having the same amount of float.

To say that all of these activities can delay their start by the amount shown would be inaccurate. Rather, the float that is shown for these activities, which is the identical value, should be shared among these activities. In other words, in many ways these activities should be treated as though they were on the critical path, because if any one of them uses the float, that will disturb the start and finish dates of the other activities in that chain. Therefore, although the total float for these activities might be six, the free float for all of them is zero. The process by which the project manager will allocate all or portions of this float to any of the activities in this chain is called "float management."

The example shown in Figure 5-14 uses the traditional schema for start and finish values. In traditional schema, the starting point of an activity is at 8 a.m. of the start day, and the end point of the activity is at 5 p.m. of the finish day. Accordingly, Element A, which has a duration of five days, has Day 1 as the earliest start day and Day 5 as the earliest finish day. Since Activity A precedes Activities B, C, F, and I, all these four activities will have the same earliest start date, i.e., Day 6.

Using the same logic, the ES and EF of all other activities are calculated. The EF calculation of Activity E, which is the last activity of the project, is particularly important. The earliest finish date of Activity E is 29, which implies that the project duration is 29 days.

Starting from Activity E and an EF value of 29 days as the basis, backward pass calculations are made (see Figure 5-13), which are shown in a separate box below each activity. The Activity E latest finish date will be same as the earliest finish date, as this is the final activity of the project. The latest start date of Activity E is derived by subtracting its duration from the project finish duration, which is 29 days; thus, the LS for Activity E is 25 days.

Since Activities B, D, H, and J are predecessors to Activity E, all will have the same latest finish date, i.e., Day 24. By subtracting its duration from 24, the LS for B, D, H, and J are calculated. Using the same logic, the LS and LF of all other activities are calculated.

After both forward pass and backward pass calculations are completed, the next step of schedule computations is to determine float for each activity. The float of an activity is calculated by subtracting the ES from the LS or the EF from the LF (see Figure 5-15). Float values shown in Figure 5-15 indicate the total float. For example, if Activity C is delayed by two days, then the ES for Activity D will change from nine to 11. However, the free float of an activity will not affect the ES of its succeeding activity.

To illustrate this concept, Activity B has 12 days of free float. By delaying it up to 12 days, the ES of Activity E will not change. Compared to Activity C, the delaying decision of Activity B will require less or no coordination with the project team.

An example of the distinction between free float and total can be found in Activities I and J. Both of them have a float of 14 days, with the implication that each one can be delayed by

14 days without affecting the project. Given that they are in a stand-alone string, they share the 14 days, and therefore the free float is zero. The project manager might choose to distribute the 14 days between these two activities, e.g., 5 and 9, or 14 and 0.

Finally, float calculations reveal the critical path of the project, which is A-F-G-H-E. All these activities have zero float, and delay in any of these activities will result in delay in the project.

SCHEDULE MANAGEMENT

Given that the same WBS is used for the formulation of the elemental cost and for the schedule network, the scope, cost, and schedule are closely integrated. Beyond that, all considerations of risk also can be incorporated into this integrated plan, during the planning phase as well as during the execution of the project. Naturally, any updates that are made to the project plans (and there should be regular and frequent updates) will be evaluated in the light of all of these integrated plans.

Resource usage over time is normally depicted in a vertical bar chart histogram and is commonly referred to as the resource histogram. With the resource requirements for each WBS element for each of the time periods of the project life cycle, and ultimately for the project, you can develop a resource histogram for each of the project's resources (see Figure 5-16). The full suite of histograms will highlight the resource requirements for all of the resources spanning the full spectrum of the project life cycle.

Resource utilization and resource histograms must take the work calendar into consideration (see Figure 5-17). As discussed in traditional schema, the traditional work calendar starts at 8 a.m. and ends at 5 p.m., including a non-working hour for lunch break, which should be taken into account for resource calculations. Likewise, working days of the week, holidays, and seasonal adjustments, which will affect productivity, also should be considered in making resource calculations.

Figure 5-16
Sample Schedule with Resource Histogram

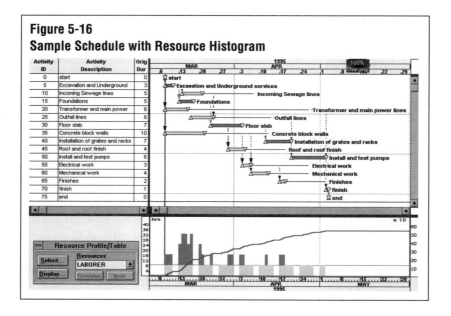

Figure 5-17
Work Calendar

- Working hours
- Non-working hours
- Working days of the week
- Holidays
- Seasonal adjustments

A major level of planning sophistication can be achieved by developing a pristine integrated plan for the project, even before overlaying the client and environmental constraints. The pristine plan would be the optimum project plan, i.e., a plan that is unencumbered with milestone constraints and low resource availability, and therefore is poised to deliver the project in the utmost efficient and cost-effective manner. By definition, a pristine schedule will not have any resource overloads because it presumes that the project can have as many resources as it needs for the optimum delivery of the project results.

Then, in response to the inevitable changes in the project environment, the project schedule would be altered to meet client requirements in resources or milestones, with possible impact on project cost. This is indicated by a company-specific optimum curve, or at least by the generic optimum curve. If the project duration needs to be compressed below the optimum duration to comply with the client's request for an early delivery date, then the resource histogram of the compressed schedule would provide an indication of the additional resources that might be necessary to effect the desired compression.

On the other hand, if there are resource limitations, you can conduct a leveling process on the network. The leveling process involves delaying activities of the project to reduce the overall resource demand for a particular resource (see Figures 5-18 and 5-19). Alternatively, if the project cannot be delayed, and if additional resources can be obtained, the histogram will help determine the amount of additional resources that would be needed.

During the project's execution period, it is very likely that costs associated with most of the resources will change from the original estimated values, which will affect project cost and may prompt initiatives to schedule changes to maintain the original cost plan. The probability of such resource cost or schedule changes is higher for projects with longer durations.

Likewise, during project execution, it is very likely that a project will experience changes in schedule due to unexpected happenings and unanticipated activities. As a result, schedules will be subjected to enhancements and updates (see Figure 5-20).

While cost and schedule changes can be triggered by enhancements and updates in deliverable information, modified client objectives also can trigger a schedule adjustment. These objectives can initially affect cost, schedule, quality, or resource availability.

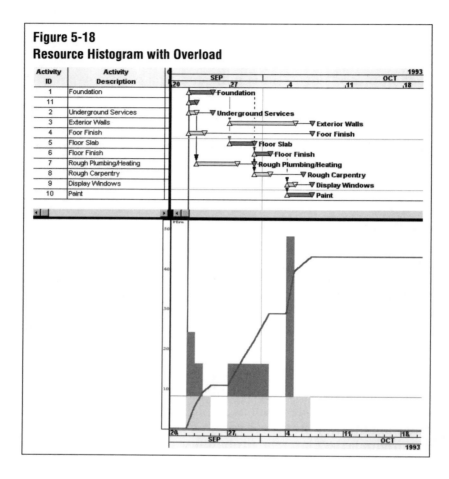

Figure 5-18
Resource Histogram with Overload

Administrative milestones often can result in durations for segments of the network that are shorter than anticipated by the current project baseline. This situation is sometimes called negative float. The remedy for a negative float situation is to implement some form of schedule compression.

At the other end of the spectrum, if the project demands more cash flow than the client can provide, then the remedy would be to expand the duration of the project in line with the client's cash flow abilities (see Figure 5-20). Expanding a schedule also will add to the project's total cost, however.

Figure 5-19
Resource Histogram Leveled

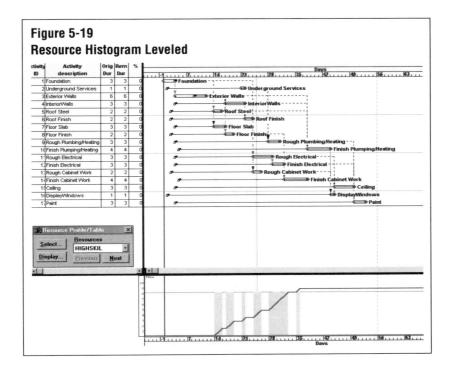

Figure 5-20
Schedule Adjustments during Maintenance Phase

- Enhancements and Updates
  - –Cost
  - –Schedule
- Constraints
  - –Administrative milestones
  - –Technical constraints
- Situations
  - –Negative float
  - –High cash flow
- Solutions
  - –Compress schedule
  - –Expand schedule

Schedule compression often is triggered by new and more constrictive client requirements for the completion date. Sometimes, when the original schedule was expanded in response to a shortage of resources, then reverting back to a shorter schedule might be regarded as compression, although in reality it is not.

Schedule compression is almost always accompanied by an increase in project cost, unless, of course, if the current baseline is an expanded form of the pristine schedule. In addition to an increase in cost, there also might be an accompanying increase in delivery risk when the project is compressed.

Since only critical path activities can be considered for compression, they must be prioritized based on the cost penalty associated with their compression. This prioritization can be on the basis of cost, risk, resources, or simply ease of compressing a particular activity. Specifically, a particular critical path element should not be considered for compression if the cost of doing so is prohibitive, if the overall schedule impact from compressing that particular element is minimal, or if the resulting risk is too high.

There are several approaches to reducing an activity's duration (see Figure 5-21). By adding more resources to an activity, its duration can be decreased. Such an approach, however, would affect productivity.

Figure 5-21
Compression Options

- Increase resources
- Change resources to more efficient resources
- Adjust work hours/extend work days
- Change technology
- Conduct fast track scheduling
- Change lead time of a major procurement
- Change supplier

Replacing existing resources with more efficient resources, such as more skilled workers and more efficient machinery, would reduce the duration to a certain extent. For this option, the project manager would need access to the organizational history for efficiency and productivity as related to skill levels.

By extending the work hours or working days in a week, you can reduce the duration of tasks, which will affect the project duration. Changes in core technologies associated with project execution also can reduce the project duration. Sometimes, it is possible to break down an activity further and then perform those fragments in parallel, thus reducing the activity's duration.

Sometimes, the delivery period of a major procurement item may lengthen the project duration. The project management team should look for an alternate supplier of the procurement item or negotiate with the supplier for speedy delivery by creating incentives.

While compressing a schedule network, keep in mind that complex networks usually have several critical paths, and, therefore, compressing activities on only one of the multiple critical paths will not reduce the duration of the project. Additionally, schedule compression will normally lead to more activities becoming critical, thus creating a highly volatile schedule. Finally, risks associated with a compressed schedule are much higher than those of a pristine schedule.

GANTT CHARTS

A Gantt chart is commonly regarded as the visual symbol of the project schedule. Although the activity interdependencies cannot be reflected accurately and conveniently in Gantt charts, a Gantt chart is easy to understand and is a good communication tool for those members of the organization who are not intimately familiar with the project.

The important distinction between the Gantt chart and the network diagram is that the former is always drawn on a time scale (see Figure 5-22), and thus the information is much easier for the reader to absorb. The network logic is sometimes drawn to a scale, but because it contains much more detailed information, it is a little harder to interpret.

A Gantt chart is a horizontal bar chart developed as a production control tool in 1917 by Henry L. Gantt, an American engineer and social scientist. Frequently used in project management, a Gantt chart provides a graphical illustration of a schedule that helps to plan, coordinate, and track specific tasks in a project. It is constructed with a horizontal axis representing time and a vertical axis representing the tasks that make up the project.

A variation of Gantt chart is a time-phased chart in which only the major milestones of the project are plotted. This chart is aptly called a milestone chart. Gantt charts and milestone charts often are used in conjunction with a network diagram to show a comprehensive suite of project information for baselines, schedule computations, and adjustments.

Scheduling is the process of calculating a project's duration, using the estimate information for WBS elements and the network logic. Other data available from the schedule network are critical path, activity floats, and resource diagrams. The network logic diagram and the duration of the activities must continually be enhanced based on more accurate information available to the project team. Further, the schedule will be modified in response to the client's current needs. The most common schedule adjustments are compression and expansion, which are caused by a need for early delivery and a constraint on resources, respectively.

Figure 5-22
Gantt Chart

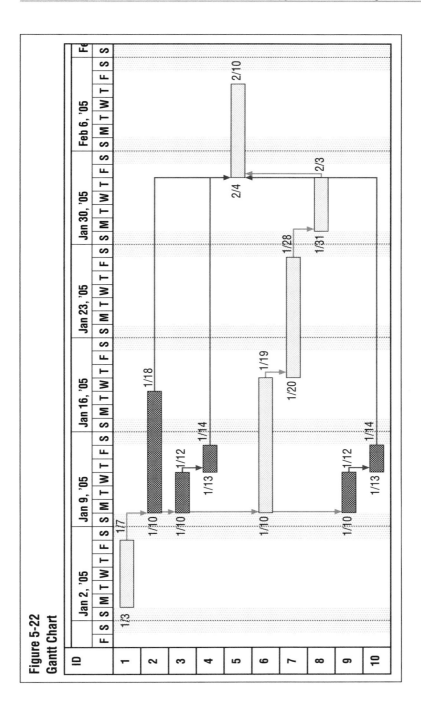

6 External Projects

For strategic reasons, organizations sometimes choose to acquire outside resources for a project. This process is called "outsourcing" or "contracting." The decision to outsource is primarily dependent on the organization's strategic objectives and is based on factors such as competencies of the prospective internal team and the infrastructure characteristics of the division sponsoring the project. Other contributing factors include market conditions and the organization's competitive aspirations.

Some organizations opt for external projects to gain immediate access to specialized skills or equipment. Others even use external projects as subtle mechanisms for transforming the culture of the organization. Finally, some organizations argue that external projects are less costly to the organization.

The disadvantage of outsourcing is that the organization will not have the opportunity to improve and enhance its own operational capability and competency. Further, the company might lose direct involvement in, and control over, execution of the project. A very important issue is that an external project might jeopardize the trade secrets and the proprietary details of the organization's best practices.

An undesirable side effect of outsourcing is that it tends to have a self-perpetuating effect on the organization, primarily because often there will be very little, if any, institutional memory from the project's execution. Therefore, the stage is set to have future projects in an outsourced mode also. Finally, the cost of executing projects outside the company can sometimes be higher if both the tangible and intangible costs are considered.

In rare cases in which the client forms partnerships with the contractor for the purposes of the project, the potential contractor is encouraged to behave as part of the same team with the client and is rewarded for behaving in the best interest of the project, although that sometimes appears to be at odds with the short-term interests of the contractor. In such cases the client tends to reap the benefits of the contractor's experience and dedication, while the contractor is allowed to earn a reasonable return on investment.

External projects often pressure the client to be more specific in defining the physical attributes and performance expectations of the final project deliverable. Ironically, it is often the scarcity of competency in the subject technical area of the project that provides the primary impetus for resorting to external projects. Therefore, providing a detailed articulation of objectives and specifications by the client might become an impossible task. As a result, in the first phase of project implementation, the contractor will need to develop the project specifications by interpreting the client's objectives.

SPECIFICATIONS

A detailed definition of the scope and objectives of the project is normally used when planning and implementing a project. Such detailed and formal specifications are frequently drafted only for external projects. However, for purposes of cost management and organizational memory, developing and maintaining specifications for internal projects as well as external projects is useful. Project specifications are included in the contract for external projects and in the authorization memo for internal projects.

Ideally, project specifications will highlight what will be delivered to the client once the project is completed. It will be less useful if the project specifications outline the activities of the project without any major emphasis on the deliverables.

The specifications documents are the most formalized articulation of the wishes and desires of the client and should include all the technical data necessary to plan and implement the project. They should provide details of all those items that are needed or desired, as well as all those that are considered undesirable or unacceptable. Further, the specifications should outline those items that are necessary for the success of the project but will be fabricated, developed, or delivered by the efforts of another project. Finally, the specifications might outline details of materials, equipment, services, procedures, and tools that should be used for the project.

The detailed information for project specifications is presented in written, tabular, and graphic formats. To some extent, the choice of the format is dictated by the nature of information. For example, graphic format is most efficient in conveying the arrangement, size, and location of physical components, while spreadsheets and tables would be the appropriate method for portraying numerical relationships. Naturally, text is most appropriate for depicting verbal description of objectives, activities, performance criteria, and strategic issues.

It is very difficult, if not virtually impossible, to produce complete and flawless specifications, as evidenced by the revisions that are issued to many contract documents even as early as during the bidding process. Therefore, you should anticipate that the specifications will change, to some extent, during the life of the project. These changes include clarifications of and modifications to the project's scope, quality, expected cost, and desired duration. As the project evolves, these changes should be reflected in the WBS, the specifications, and other planning documents.

To facilitate comprehension of and compliance with the specifications, all facets of the project deliverables must be quantified, to the extent practicable. Accordingly, attempts should be made to quantify deliverable qualifiers such as user-friendly, robust, smooth, and aesthetically pleasing.

There are three types of specifications: focused design, generic performance, and functional. Focused design, or product, specifications provide details of what is to be delivered in terms of physical characteristics, or in terms of detailed tasks intended to contribute to a product or a service. An example of this type of specification is when the client provides details of how web pages should be designed, what graphics should be used in the various web pages, and how many records the database should contain. As such, the risk of performance and applicability rests directly with the client (see Figure 6-1).

If the specifications are drafted with performance, or generic, characteristics in mind, they define measurable operational capabilities that the deliverable must achieve. An example of this type of specification is when the client spells out the access speed, error rate, and general linkage characteristics of the website. The project team will then draft plans that will have the proper technical features so that the deliverable will satisfy the client's performance expectations. Naturally, the risk of performance is borne by the project team, while the risk of applicability is borne by the client (see Figure 6-2).

Figure 6-1
Focused Design Specifications

- Provide details of deliverable's physical characteristics
- Place risk of performance and applicability on client

Figure 6-2
Generic Performance Specifications

- Specify measurable capabilities that deliverable must achieve in terms of operational characteristics
- Project team has some discretion in crafting deliverable
- Place risk of performance on project team
- Place risk of applicability on client

Functional specifications are usually the most logical mode of responding to the "wants and needs" of the client. However, they burden the client with the task of defining, in very clear terms, the basic objective of the final product. At the same time, this mode of specification development will empower the project team to use creative and innovative techniques to meet or exceed the client's expectations (see Figure 6-3).

An example of this type of specification is when the client provides the contractor with the general business plan and the expected business outcome. The contractor then will develop a set of detailed plans and specifications that will enable the project to meet those business needs. Under this mode of operation, it is entirely possible that the contractor will communicate the specifications to the client, but that is usually just to keep the client informed and not necessarily for approval purposes.

In some cases, the client and the project team collectively develop project specifications. In other cases, such as in software and system development projects, the implementation team develops the project specifications by interpreting and analyzing the client's needs and objectives. As much as such collaboration is very useful, it has the risk of blending project specifications with project implementation details and with project scheduling techniques.

This practice also blurs the line between the client's goals and the project team's objectives. Analyzing and evaluating the causes of cost and duration overruns can be very difficult if

---

Figure 6-3
Functional Specifications

- Describe deliverable's end use
- Stimulate creativity of team members
- Provide environment for novel solutions
- Place risk of performance and applicability on project team

there is an overlap between client-generated material and contractor-generated material.

Finally, cost and duration overruns usually are accompanied by a gradual change in project scope, thus complicating the identification of a logical baseline for the project. If the scope changes are not documented, or if they are not managed in a formalized and consistent fashion, one more level of difficulty will be added to the task of managing the resulting cost impact of the schedule and scope changes to the project.

This continuous shifting of the baseline is sometimes referred to as scope creep. Scope creep is endemic in projects that are conducted as cost plus or in organizations that have very few original project objectives, or in projects whose plans and specifications have been formulated on the basis of objectives that can be characterized as "fuzzy." However, it is fair to say that a certain amount of scope modification should be expected in most projects, both external and internal.

CONTRACTS

Although many external projects are initiated with the execution of a contract, and although many projects will need contracts to acquire resources and deliverables, a project should be treated as the legal instrument by which an organization acquires products and services from an outside source. For the purposes of managing a successful project, a contract is considered an administrative mechanism by which the project is conducted by personnel who reside outside the corporate boundaries of the client organization (see Figure 6-4).

Figure 6-4
Contract (Casual Definition)

A binding agreement to acquire goods and services

Even when the project would not exist if it were not for the contract, the contract can be viewed as an expanded and highly formalized adaptation of the project charter. Notwithstanding, to define the responsibilities and rewards of both parties, a contract must conform to the legal definition of a contract, as shown in Figure 6-5. It is in the light of these considerations that a contract is drafted, signed, and enforced. The contractor's offer is called a bid and, when chosen for the job, is referred to as the winner of the contract.

Contract documents for a project are composed of two major parts: administrative and technical. The administrative part deals with the legal responsibilities of both parties and with processes and procedures for enforcing the various contract clauses. The second part deals with the technical content of the project. This part of the contract is—or should be—the most important part to the project team, since it spells out the specifications, performance expectations, and delivery constraints of the deliverable (see Figure 6-6).

There are two basic forms of project contracts, as shown in Figure 6-7. The first type is called fixed price or lump sum. This type of contract requires detailed specifications. Usually, the contractor who offers the lowest price will be chosen for that particular project. In this mode of contracting, the prospective contractor offers to deliver the project deliverables for a fixed price. The contractor guarantees the fixed price and thus assumes all financial risk in implementing that project—that is, of course, if the initial set of client objectives and project speci-

Figure 6-5
Contract (Legal Definition)

- An understanding enforceable by law
- Between two or more parties
- For money or for exchange
- Substance should be legal
- Requires an offer and an acceptance

Figure 6-6
Contract Documents

- Envision all physical and *administrative* possibilities, set guidelines
  –General conditions
  –Special conditions
- Present *technical* data for this job
  –Text
  –Tabular
  –Graphic

Figure 6-7
Types of Contracts

- Lump sum (fixed price)
- Cost plus fixed fee (time and material)

fications are spelled out with sufficient detail and if the project environment remains reasonably stable during the life of the project. Under ideal circumstances, this type of contract gives the contractor full incentives to avoid waste, to reduce costs, and to increase profits (see Figure 6-8).

Again, the lump sum contract is most appropriate for projects with precisely outlined scope and specifications that have little chance of changing (see Figure 6-9). If there are midstream changes to the scope and specifications, the contract will be modified to reflect a new price. The new price, and other conditions of the contract, will be negotiated between the contractor and the client at the onset of these changes in the project environment. The advisability of the lump sum type of contract will come under scrutiny during, and as a result of, these contract modifications.

The second type of contract is called cost plus, or time-and-materials. In this form of contracting, the contractor is selected on the basis of technical capability as well as on the basis of charging the lowest amount of money per unit of labor, equipment, overhead, and materials. The owner then directs the

---

Figure 6-8
Lump-Sum Contract

- Requires accurate and detailed design
- Minimizes initial uncertainties in cost and quality

Figure 6-9
Characteristics of Lump-Sum Contract

- Safe for the owner
  —If the scope stays unchanged
- Low profits for the contractor
  —If the scope stays unchanged
- Potentially explosive for both
  —If the scope is changed

---

contractor to perform the various tasks of the project, while the contractor is paid for actual expenditures in accordance with the client's instructions (see Figure 6-10), plus a fee. The reimbursable costs include labor, equipment, materials, and possibly service and supply subcontracts.

In construction and industrial projects, there is a third basic form of contracting, which is called unit price (see Figure 6-11). This form is a mixture of the two basic forms described above. In effect, unit price represents a fixed price for a small element of the project. Under this type of a contract, the contractor submits a bid for each of the many small elements of the project. Then the contractor gets paid for the number of these units that are used for the project. Examples of unit pricing elements include one specific test using one specific testing machine, one line of code, one web page, one yard of concrete, one module of training, one hour of an engineer, and one hour of a programmer.

Experience has shown that these basic forms of contracting do not address challenges that present themselves during the life of the projects, such as scope changes, environmental changes, and design changes. Consequently, organizations award

---

Figure 6-10
Characteristics of Cost-Plus Contract

- Contractor's profit is always protected
- Gives the owner freedom to modify scope frequently
- Project estimate becomes a vague target
- Little incentive for contractor to be productive or efficient

---

Figure 6-11
Types of Contracts

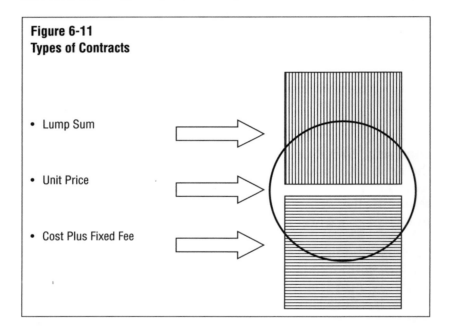

- Lump Sum

- Unit Price

- Cost Plus Fixed Fee

---

contracts that use one of the basic forms with modifiers that reward or restrict the behavior of the contractor. Examples of these modifiers are shown in Figure 6-12.

Modifiers are intended to give the client the flexibility to modify the project specifications midstream in a way that has the lowest possible impact on project cost and duration. They are also intended to provide incentives to the contractor to be efficient, responsive, and exceptionally mindful of the best interests of the client—not to the exclusion, of course, of the contractor's objectives of receiving the highest possible return on investment.

Figure 6-12
Contract Modifiers (for Cost-Plus or Unit-Cost Contracts)

- Guaranteed maximum
- Overrun cost sharing
- Underrun profit sharing
- Bonus for underrun
- Penalty for overrun
- Bonus for early delivery
- Penalty for late delivery
- Reduced fee for being late or over budget
- No fee after estimated date and cost

The contract management procedures should outline the process for developing specifications, selecting contract type, and source selection. Additionally, these procedures should outline procedures for monitoring the contractor's performance within the boundaries established by the contract and in light of the project's technical objectives. While contract management planning documents should include procedures and policies to ensure contract compliance, they also should afford a reasonable amount of flexibility for minor changes in the deliverables.

RESPONSE TO SPECIFICATIONS

The role of specifications is minimal in cost-plus contracts, and there is no need to develop them fully during the contract award phase because the contractor will be paid based on how much time and effort is spent rather than on what is produced. In most cases, a cost-plus contractor is chosen on the basis of perceived capability and potential reliability, and not necessarily on a promised total cost or delivery date. Given the nature of the cost-plus contracts, sometimes the first assignment of the contractor is to develop the specifications and estimates for the project, and it is almost certain that the same contractor will implement the resulting specifications.

On the other hand, the role of specifications is pivotal in fixed-price contracts because the specifications will form the basis for the estimate, bid, and eventual award. Modifying a fixed-price contract midstream is difficult, time-consuming, and potentially expensive. Therefore, fixed-price contracts should be awarded only if the specifications are exceptionally accurate and if the probability of changes in the specifications is extraordinarily low.

When reviewing specifications, the project manager must make every effort to understand all of the client's objectives and underlying reasons for wanting particular facets of the deliverable. Then, the project manager must make every effort to meet all the needs of the client cost-effectively. Ideally, this philosophy should be the guiding light for all types of projects because it fosters client-contractor partnership and trust.

Unfortunately, this philosophy is not practiced widely in contracting environments because it subtly affects the contracting strategy, bidding outcomes, and award circumstances. Although implementing such a congenial and trusting environment is possible, it must be approached with some sensitivity to the fact that the obligations and the reward system for the contractor personnel and client personnel, as delineated by the contract, are different and possibly in conflict.

Partly prompted by competitive contracting strategy, and partly in an effort to portray a tendency to be accommodating, prospective fixed-price contractors often offer to comply with all the conditions set forth in contract specifications, even if the contractor suspects that the client's specifications are flawed. The reinforcing element for this behavior is that the clients often regard such conformist behavior positively. Notwithstanding, if there are changes to the project scope during the life of the project, such changes would be grounds for renegotiating the contract, usually to a higher price.

It is not known how many contractors could have predicted the nature and extent of the scope changes of a contract but chose not to confront the client about the quality of the specifications. However, it is commonly accepted that contractors of fixed-price contracts tend to prosper when there are many change orders during the life of the contract.

Ideally, when a set of specifications is presented to the project manager or to a potential contractor, and if there are flaws or omissions in the statements of scope, specifications, or desired procedures, the contractor or project manager should ethically and logically respond in any or all of the ways listed in Figure 6-13. Such responses will serve the best interests of the client, while also serving the best long-term interests of the contractor.

Sometimes, however, there is a conflict between the contractor's short-term and long-term interests. The recommended responses are to ask questions when there is ambiguity, to list assumptions when the specifications are incomplete, to take exception when an objective is unattainable, and to make suggestions when the specifications need improvements.

Figure 6-13
Response to Client's Requirements

- Ask questions
  - –Smart questions
  - –Dumb questions
- List assumptions
  - –Develop lists for
    - Inclusions
    - Exclusions
    - Deliverables of other groups needed for this project
- Take exception
  - –Let client know that
    - The approach is impossible
    - The deliverable is unattainable
- Make suggestions
  - –Highlight your expertise by offering alternatives

Traditionally, contractors' responses are more in line with compliance rather than the seemingly confrontational responses outlined in Figure 6-13. In some cases, the clients reinforce the contractor's passive behavior by rewarding those who exhibit non-feedback and by punishing those who provide feedback that is not entirely complimentary (see Figure 6-14).

BIDDING

A bid and an estimate are two entirely different things, although sometimes clients and contractors use these two terms interchangeably. An estimate is a detailed account of the cost of delivering a product based on specific information about the actual cost of materials and equipment, on the actual salary of personnel, and on a realistic characterization of the overhead structure of the contractor's organization; in other words, an estimate will reflect the real cost of a project. Depending on the circumstances, an estimate may or may not include overhead costs, indirect costs, and profit.

By comparison, the bid or contract price may not necessarily include details of the various components of the cost estimate that have formed the basis for the bid. Even if the bid does

---

Figure 6-14
Consequences (Responding to Client Requirements)

- *The entrepreneurial approach is to provide feedback in all four categories*
  - If your response uncovers a flaw in the client's original communication, or sheds light on alternatives, you might be rewarded by the client
  - However, if this response indicates lack of planning or knowledge on your part, your image might be tarnished

- *The safe approach is to give minimal feedback*
  - You will not create an impression of competency with the client—neither favorable nor unfavorable
  - The stellar facets of your experience and performance will remain undiscovered

include details of components such as direct costs, indirect costs, overhead, contingency, and return on investment, these figures might not be actual or realistic.

The amounts included in a bid simply represent the amounts that the contractor is planning to charge for labor, materials and equipment, indirect costs, overhead costs, contingencies, and the all-important return on investment. These values usually are developed for the purposes of the bid. The transition from an estimate to a bid is a business decision that is based on the probability of desirable or undesirable unexpected events occurring and on the bidder's motivation to acquire this contract.

Generally, the profit margin in a contract must be in concert with the number of bidders for the same job, primarily because the prospective contractors, in an effort to be the lowest bidder, will reduce the overall profit to its lowest possible margin. As Figure 6-15 shows, when there are a lot of bidders for the same job, the expected profit margin is very low; for jobs with very few bidders, the profit margin will increase accordingly (DeNeufville and Hani 1977; Gates 1978). The most desirable situation for a contractor, clearly, is one in which there are very few bidders for the contract.

A low profit margin will increase the chances of being the successful bidder, although bidding a job below realistic cost does not necessarily guarantee wining the contract. On the other hand, an extraordinarily high profit margin might reduce the chances of being the successful bidder, although bidding a job with high profit margin does not necessarily eliminate all chances of wining the contract.

The presence of a contract creates an environment of delineated objectives that sometimes precludes a common focus on the project by the client and the contractor. Various efforts in the areas of partnering have established a less adversarial contract environment, but keep in mind that contractors and clients have different sets of motivations and objectives.

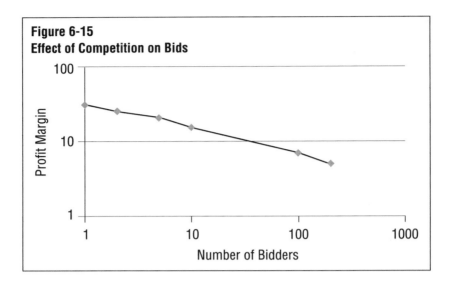

Figure 6-15
Effect of Competition on Bids

In a contracting situation, the bidder's objectives are to win the contract, complete the project quickly, receive prompt payment, and make a good profit. On the other hand, the owner's objectives are to pay the lowest price possible for the earliest delivery date and to receive a responsive performance. The number of lawsuits that clients and contractors file against one another demonstrates this adversarial attitude, which stems from the disparity between the client's business objectives and the contractor's operating objectives.

PROJECT COSTS

Normally when an internal project is commissioned, the cost of the project does not include anything beyond the cost of assigning personnel and equipment—sometimes not even the cost of equipment. However, the real cost of the project includes other cost components such as labor, equipment, materials, indirect costs, overhead, and return on investment.

The distinctions among direct cost, indirect cost, and overhead tend to be more important in organizations that conduct external projects. A sensitivity to the issues of indirect and overhead costs will allow an internal project manager to assess the real cost of an internal project and to compare two internal projects on the basis of direct costs. When comparing an external project with an internal project, care should be taken to include the necessary additional direct cost items of the internal project.

Direct Costs

Direct costs are those costs that are directly attributable to the project, such as personnel salaries, travel, and cost of buying or renting equipment for the explicit use of the project. One popular way of testing the direct cost elements is to consider the costs of those people and equipment that actually came in contact with the project deliverable, and for what duration. It is important to remember that if personnel or equipment are shared between projects, only the portion of the salary and purchase costs that were used for the activities of a particular project should be included.

Indirect Costs

Indirect costs include the costs of infrastructure and human and physical resources necessary for the project to operate smoothly, again to the extent that the resources were indirectly associated with the project. Indirect costs include the cost of items such as sick leave, vacation, training, Social Security contributions, health care, and retirement benefits for employees. Indirect costs also will include portions of the salary of supervisory personnel who support the project. Other indirect items are portions of the cost of administrative support, the phone system, faxes, computers, rent, insurance, taxes, and utilities.

Direct costs and indirect costs are items that can easily be related to the cost of implementing components of the deliverables. They are an integral part of the cost estimate of an external project and therefore should not be allowed to become subject to negotiations or alterations during the contract award phases.

Overhead

Overhead items are somewhat removed from the project, although they are necessary to conduct it successfully. They include compensation for the organization's senior management and the cost of the infrastructure necessary to support their activities. Overhead items also include the cost of preparing unsuccessful proposals, general marketing and public relations, research and development for capability improvement, and ongoing innovative business ventures of the organization.

The extent to which these overhead costs should be charged to a project is always the subject of extensive debate between clients and contractors. This loosely knit bundle of cost categories is always under scrutiny by the prospective client, and therefore it is an issue of negotiation at the time of the award for a contract for an external project. Finally, a project is very unattractive if it does not produce a profit or return on investment.

The extent of return on investment is another issue of contract negotiation. The return on investment should provide a very strong motivation to the contractor for undertaking the project, unless the contractor is so desperate that he or she is willing to settle just for cash flow, or even for a slight loss.

Allowance

An allowance is a lump-sum estimate that is assigned to certain project items. It is somewhat akin to an analogous estimate for that particular component of the project. Usually, the basis for using an allowance for an item instead of a detailed estimate is that although the project manager predicts that a certain cost will be incurred, he or she also has determined that the elements cannot be identified with any accuracy or that a detailed tabulation is not necessary because the item is very small in comparison with other WBS elements.

An example of an allowance is the estimate for travel expenses. If the project manager knows that it is likely that the team might have to travel to the installation sites about a dozen times, he or she includes an allowance of $75,000 for travel expenses rather than estimating the cost of airline tickets and hotel costs for each separate trip. Other examples include the cost of office supplies, phone calls, and software licenses. An allowance should be used very infrequently, and even then only for those cost elements that comprise a very small percentage of the project's overall cost.

Contingency

The terms "contingency" and "client reserve" often are used interchangeably, but they refer to two different kinds of buffer funds. In some ways, contingency funds and reserve funds are akin to allowances, except that contingency funds and reserve funds deal with unknown issues and issues outside the contract price structure. Sometimes, clients establish contingency and reserve funds even for internal projects, to put some formality in budget development.

For the purposes of this book, the term "contingency" is used for the funds that are added to the estimate to compensate for inaccuracies caused by uncertainties in project details. The term "client reserve" refers to those funds that are set aside to subsidize the cost changes brought on by expansions of client objectives, environmental changes, and sometimes client-directed design changes. Client reserve funds refer to those funds that are set aside by the client as part of the organizational budget, but apart from the contract budget.

The definition and purpose of contingency and reserve funds will become blurred if there are regular, or occasional, changes to the project scope during the life of the contract. The definition becomes even more blurred if the risk-related contingency funds are rolled together with client reserve funds in the same account. Contingency funds are not to be used to cover the cost of errors in design, implementation, or omission, or those caused by miscalculation in estimating. These items should be addressed as part of a renegotiation for or amendments of a new budget or contract.

Traditionally, the magnitude of contingency funds is from 10 percent to 50 percent of total project funds, depending on the volume of information available at the time of the estimate. This range is deemed appropriate because it is generally anticipated that when a project is advertised for bid, the objectives and statements of specification possess a reasonable accuracy of about 20 percent.

The magnitude of client reserve funds varies from 10 percent to 50 percent of the total project funds, depending on the level of innovation required in the project, which in turn might trigger major design changes (Anonymous[1] 2000; Anonymous[2] 1999; Anonymous[5] 1999; Vigder and Kark 1994). The level of client reserves also depends on the extent to which the client team, who developed the estimate, was familiar with cutting-edge developments in the area.

PROJECT AUDIT

If the organization hosting the project is highly sophisticated, it will conduct regular project reviews, and most of the stakeholders and all of the team members will be aware of the real status of the project. The regular project reviews might be performed by a central unit, such as a project management office (PMO).

Formalized audits will be unnecessary for projects or organizations that practice regular and detailed project monitoring, thereby giving a clear picture of the status of projects at all times. However, less enlightened organizations are not always aware of the status of all projects at all times. Therefore, occasional or regular formal project audits may be necessary to assess the real status of the project.

The usefulness of the project deliverables and the progress of the project's implementation often are evaluated using a formal project audit. A project audit is different from a financial audit in that it concentrates on all project attributes, a small portion of which include the cost performance attributes.

The project progress attributes to be audited should include those that measure the pace of progress in terms of achieving the intermediate milestones, the cost of delivered items, and the quality or performance of the deliverables as compared with the most recent baseline. The audit also may take into account the behavior of contractor personnel, such as responsiveness and attitude. Ideally, the audit procedures for an outsourced project will focus on the same indicators that are normally monitored during the progress-monitoring phase of an internal project.

If the result of the audit shows that the project cost and schedule are out of control, and therefore completing the project will be far more costly or much later than anticipated, then the project might need to be terminated (see Figure 6-16). If the results of an audit, viewed in light of the current organizational strategic direction, deem an internal project no longer necessary or viable, that project can be terminated with reasonable ease. The personnel and equipment that were assigned to this internal project can then be dispersed through the organization somewhat systematically (see Figure 6-17).

Figure 6-16
Project Termination Types

- Pleasant and predictable
  –Project requirements have been met
- Unpleasant and somewhat unexpected
  –Some assumptions have proven to be false
  –Performance is inadequate
  –Project deliverables are no longer desired
  –Time and money issues (most frequent causes)

Unless the external project is being terminated due to the poor performance of the contractor in any of the triple-constraint areas, and therefore in breach of the contract, terminating an external project is far more complex and costly than terminating an internal project. If the contractor is progressing in a reasonably satisfactory pace at the time the external project is terminated, then the client will negotiate to compensate the contractor for the cost of completed work, work in progress, mobilization for future tasks, early demobilization costs, and anticipated profits.

Figure 6-17
Scheduled Termination

- Review entire project
- Conduct detailed closeout
- Write final report
- Ensure that documentation is in good order
- Account for and reassign resources
- Meet with customers to see whether their needs have been addressed
- Prepare for handover of the deliverable

If the project cannot be conveniently conducted within the organization, then an outside organization can be delegated to implement it. External projects add value to an organization quickly and without major administrative disturbance, although there is an ongoing debate as to whether external projects are cost-effective. Additionally, some argue that external projects deflect any risks that might have affected the funding organization, while others argue that external projects bring their own brand of risks to the organization, particularly financial ones.

If the project has been clearly and carefully defined, then a fixed-price contract is appropriate. Otherwise, a service contract, usually known as cost-plus-fee contract, is more appropriate. Independent of the mode of contracting, the client often is placed in a position of making tradeoff decisions. Therefore, the client should make every effort to monitor the progress of the project closely to be prepared to deal with any unexpected events.

7 Progress Monitoring

Monitoring project performance is essential to keeping the project manager informed of the status of the deliverable. Data collected during the process is crucial in managing the issues and circumstances that will be brought on by the inevitable changes to the project.

The focus and emphasis of project progress monitoring is fundamentally different from traditional cost accounting. Cost accounting by and large deals with issues involved in reporting the expenses to the correct components of the established budget cost centers and account codes. Cost accounting focuses on collecting accurate actual cost information with specific attention to the elements of the code of accounts; project progress monitoring, on the other hand, focuses on areas of resource expenditure as delineated by the WBS.

There is no question that accurate collection of cost information should be part of the data that are collected or computed by a project monitoring system. However, cost is not the primary concern of the project management data collection; rather, deliverable-specific resource expenditure data are the key concern. There is also a belief that cost accounting, by and large, focuses on history, whereas project monitoring collects data for improving performance and for predicting the future.

The observed variances in resource expenditure, cost, and project duration will be used to identify trends, which will in turn be used to make midcourse adjustments to project plans. Depending on the organization, these adjustments might or might not result in a new budget, but at the very least a realistic prediction of these values for project completion will be developed. The reliance on the RBS and WBS, provided by a formalized progress monitoring system, will allow project managers to compile meaningful historical data that will be useful in managing the changes in the texture of the current project, while providing useful historical data for streamlining the estimation and management of future projects.

The accuracy and efficiency of the project estimate depends on data collected from previous experiences in similar projects, and in turn a formalized monitoring system will produce a new set of data. These data will be very useful in collecting historical data for cost estimating models and general organizational memory, which will in turn benefit the effectiveness of future projects. In essence, although the progress monitoring system benefits the project at hand significantly, it has far-reaching benefits for future projects and for organizational project management effectiveness as a whole.

Progress monitoring is most successful when it is fully embedded into the formalized organizational procedures for managing projects. Therefore, progress-monitoring procedures should be part of the organizational project management culture, rather than narrowly focused just on the project at hand.

The progress monitoring system should be formulated and implemented so that it will not negatively affect the efficiency, creativity, innovation, and morale of the project team's technical personnel. Rather, it must be a facilitative tool that informs the team members of their individual assignments, reminds them of forthcoming events, and warns of significant variances. Additionally, the progress monitoring system will centrally store the data for forecasting and future customization of estimating models.

Unfortunately, in many of the creativity-based and highly specialized projects, the project team might regard progress reporting as cumbersome, intrusive, and a signal that senior management does not trust the project team. Project managers who use progress data for pressuring individual task leaders to deliver products faster often reinforce and perpetuate these sentiments. Further, divisional managers who, with a misguided objective of efficiency and improvement, use progress data to micromanage the project team provide unwitting affirmation of the team's negative attitude toward progress monitoring measures.

The function of a progress monitoring system is to keep each project team member informed of the progress of his or her own task and apprised of the progress toward attainment of the overall objectives by all of the team members. As such, the progress monitoring system should be regarded as nothing other than a valuable aid.

In other instances, particularly in projects that involve a great deal of creativity and new technology, project team members regard progress monitoring as an affront to creativity. Ironically, a logical progress monitoring system should not impede creativity, but rather should assist the team members in understating the cost and schedule implications of their contributions to the project, thus allowing the project professionals to concentrate on producing superior deliverables. With proper education, the majority of the team members and upper management should adopt a more accurate view of progress monitoring.

If the organization is progressive enough to have a PMO, much of the formalization of the progress reporting process is handled as part of its foundation. Although many organizations do in fact have a project management culture and a commitment to formalized project management, this organizational entity may not be called a PMO. The qualities that are necessary to achieve the desired goals in project management are: organizational commitment to project management principles, a set of consistent procedures, and a battery of operational tools (see Figure 7-1).

The basic foundation for a project management culture is the firm commitment to principles of project management, such

---

Figure 7-1
Implementation Elements

- Project management principles
- Consistent procedures
- Facilitative tools

---

as formal scope definition for every project, extensive use of the major project structures, logical cost management policies, and usable cost reporting procedures (see Figure 7-2). The commitment to these principles should be reinforced by the use of enterprise guidelines and procedures such as those necessary for superior performance in project initiation, approval, mobilization, implementation, and closeout (see Figure 7-3).

Figure 7-2
Project Management Principles

- Define project objective and scope
- Develop project execution plan
- Identify WBS, RBS, and OBS
- Organize budget and schedule
- Develop progress reporting schemes
- Formulate analysis criteria
- Establish monitoring guidelines
- Manage unexpected changes

Figure 7-3
Project Management Consistent Procedures

- Project approval
- Scope development
- Budget preparation and approval
- Project mobilization
- Progress reporting
- Management of change
- Collection of historical data

Finally, the project team members must have at their disposal a set of operational tools that facilitate compliance with enterprise project management policies. These tools, which must be updated and expanded regularly to stay at the state of the art, include data capture forms, scheduling methodologies, progress reporting forms, and performance enhancing software packages such as PM software, databases, spreadsheets, and presentation graphics (see Figure 7-4).

The project monitoring policies and tools are not meant to be restrictive, but rather informative and facilitative. To that end, as the organization matures, and as highly competent project teams contribute to designing and conducting the monitoring process, the suitability, applicability, and usability of the project management tools and techniques will continually improve.

DEVELOP A MONITORING PLAN

The project monitoring system must be appropriate to the project and to the environment that hosts it. This appropriateness can be ensured by defining, clarifying, and documenting the unique attributes of the project and the organization. The procedures by which projects are initiated also should include procedures for establishing baselines and for monitoring the project against them.

Figure 7-4
Project Management Operational Tools

- Data capture forms
- CPM and PERT methodology
- Software packages
  - –Project management
  - –Database manipulation
  - –Presentation graphics
- Progress reports
- Progress meetings

Normally, those people at the higher levels of the corporate structure authorize the vision for a new project or a new corporate initiative (see Figure 7-5). Such a vision might emanate either from the upper levels of the organization or, in more enlightened organizations, be developed at the project level and presented to upper management for approval. As the implementation of this initiative is delegated to lower levels of the organization, a more detailed definition of this vision is developed.

The directive that is drafted at the CEO level may be a one-paragraph or even a one-line vision (see Figure 7-6). However, by the time this initiative is developed at the lower levels of the organization, it may involve many pages of descriptive design and many pages of hardware and software specifications. To use WBS terminology here, the Level Zero of the project is specified at the top levels of the organization, and the lower levels are developed, designed, and implemented by the subsequent levels of the organization through the project team members.

Figure 7-5
Project Stakeholders

President
Division Vice President
Manager of Projects
Project Manager
Senior Project Planner
Project Staff

Figure 7-6
Project Plans

Concept
Concept Concept
Concept Strategy Concept
Strategy Concept Plan Strategy
Plan Plan Strategy Plan Plan Strategy
Detailed Plan Detailed Plan Detailed Plan

Voluminous and detailed project data are exceptionally useful to the project team members but can be overwhelming to those who are not intimately involved with the project. Likewise, during project implementation and when the progress data are compiled, refined, and tabulated, care should be taken to observe the same level of detail in the refinement or analysis of the data that is contained in the reports that will be distributed.

The best data collection and reporting systems are those that customize the level of detail to the organizational stature, and involvement level, of the person supplying the information for the report and the person receiving the report. Additionally, the data that are collected, and the trends that are reported, must be at a level of detail that allows deviations of the actual value from the baseline project plan to be detected. Finally, the report frequency must be such that the project team can deploy corrective measures in a timely and useful manner if the variances indicate the need for a change in the project's pace.

Project staff members should get all possible details regarding their own tasks, interdependent tasks, and the project in general. However, at the other end of the spectrum, the CEO probably will get a one- or two-line report on the status of the cost and schedule of the project—maybe not even at the same frequency that the team gets its reports. Naturally, if any of the top executives require additional information for a more detailed review, it can be made available (see Figure 7-7).

Figure 7-7
Data and Report

```
                          Report
                      Report  Report
                  Report  Analyze  Report
              Analyze  Report  Capture  Analyze
          Capture  Capture  Analyze  Capture  Analyze
      Capture  Capture  Capture  Capture  Capture  Capture
```

The same degree of specificity that was used in generating the project definition documents must be applied to defining the contents and distribution pattern of the progress reports. The progress monitoring procedures must specify how often the data capture should be conducted for the progress reports and how often the progress reports should be issued.

When developing data capture procedures, all affected parties must agree on who will collect the data, who will provide it, and what the expected tolerance of the data is (see Figure 7-8). For example, if the item to be measured is the number of programs written or volume of concrete poured, the project charter must specify whether the measurement is to be performed by the technical person doing the work or by an administrative staff person who is in charge of data collection. Beyond that, specifics of the frequency of data collection must be outlined beforehand (e.g., if the data will be collected, daily, weekly, monthly, or quarterly).

Those project stakeholders who receive progress reports should be fully aware of their obligations regarding the contents of the report. Some may receive the report for information only, and no action is required of them. Others may receive the report for review and action. The type of action and the turnaround time must be specified as part of the project charter or the monitoring guidelines (see Figure 7-9). This kind of specificity ultimately will introduce efficiency and expediency in the conduct of the project.

Figure 7-8
Data Capture Projects

- Who will collect the data?
- Who will provide the data?
- How often?
  - –Every day
  - –Each Monday
  - –First day of month
  - –First day of quarter
- What is the expected tolerance of the data?

Figure 7-9
Report Distribution List

- Frequency of report distribution
  –Daily, Monday, monthly, quarterly
- Personnel receiving the report for information only
- Personnel receiving the report for action
  –Action type:
    • Phone turnaround, input sheet, meeting, memo, letter, report
  –Urgency:
    • Action expected within hours/days/weeks/months

With these precautions in place, the volume of a progress report will not overwhelm the recipients when their involvement
in the project is minimal. Further, there will be fewer occasions
when someone is not sure why he or she has received a progress report. More to the point, those who need to react to the
project events will get the correct and sufficient information to
execute their specific duties.

If these steps are implemented in the reporting system, project
personnel will know what is expected of them in terms of data
to be provided for input into the progress reporting system.
Accordingly, the project personnel will have a clear picture of
the volume, quality, and frequency of the reports they will be
receiving.

To increase the monitoring and reporting system's utility, the
collected data must be compiled and refined as part of each
data collection cycle. Then, the refined data and their analysis
should be reported to the team in a timely manner, and at the
level of detail that is useful to the recipients.

DETAILS OF MONITORING

Examples of progress indicators in construction projects are
number of feet of wire pulled, cubic yards of concrete poured,
and square feet of carpet installed. Examples of progress indices in systems development projects are number of screens

completed, number of lines of code written, and number of machines enabled. For WBS elements that have a series of sequential subtasks, the achieved milestones can be a measure of progress. Examples of task milestones for a server installation project could be receive, place, connect, test, accept, and turnover.

In some organizational environments, lapsed time and cost of labor are considered indications of progress. Although these indicators are useful in measuring the cost incurred, they do not have a direct relationship with progress, and therefore they can be misleading and highly inaccurate for reporting progress.

A more rational set of progress indices would include measurements of what has been delivered and indications of the rate of resource expenditures with respect to each deliverable. The raw progress data for each activity should contain as many of the following pieces of information as possible: actual start date of the activity, volume of deliverables, effort spent so far, and effort needed to finish the activity.

The raw data, by which progress in activities of the project will be recorded, might also include work days spent, worker days spent, total cost of labor, and total cost of materials or equipment (see Figure 7-10). Care must be taken to distinguish between worker days, workdays, and lapsed days when capturing progress data.

Figure 7-10
Progress Reporting

- Measurable
  - –Volume of deliverables
  - –Effort spent so far
  - –Hours spent on deliverable
  - –Work days lapsed
  - –Effort needed to finish activity

The progress monitoring system provides formalized data capture procedures that will allow development of a set of logical and rational indices to measure the pace of attaining project objectives. The progress is measured in the areas of cost, schedule, and scope. The baseline data might be the original baseline data, although in most cases they are a modified version of the original. To clarify, the purpose of progress monitoring is not to force project progress, and its associated costs, to the figures that were pre-defined as part of the plans and budget, but rather to report accurate values of actual project performance indices, with the hope of developing work-arounds for the significant variances.

The project manager might use the progress data as a basis for making adjustments to the work pace. Alternately, he or she may make an informed determination that the variances are transient or not significant, and that no major changes need to be made. Finally, the project manager might conclude that it is more appropriate to draft a budget modification request.

EARNED VALUE

The general definition of earned value, in the context of project management, is a definitive indication of how much progress has been made in delivering the final project results. In the case of external fixed-price projects, this value translates to the amount of funds that are payable to the contractor.

Calculating earned value has been found to be a very effective tool in measuring the progress of contractors in external projects. Computing earned value can be part of an audit activity, or it can be integrated into the project's progress monitoring system.

The concept of earned value generally is used in monitoring the progress of fixed-price contracts in which the objective is to calculate the amount of payment that is due to the contractor. The values derived using this concept will highlight the

portion of the payment that the contractor has earned by calculating the amount of deliverables produced as of the reporting date. However, to the extent that earned value reflects the
magnitude of progress, it also will be useful in internal projects. It can serve as an equally powerful tool in determining
the rate of progress of internal projects toward achieving the
goals of the project.

For creativity-based tasks, in which the deliverable often defies
measurement and in which progress is an illusive and immea-
surable concept, guidelines need to be established for measuring the project's progress. Depending on the organizational
culture, project complexity, and the needs of the project, one
of several crediting methods can be applied.

For some activities, progress credit can be applied when the
task is started, and credit can be applied incrementally as
progress is made. Yet, in other organizational environments,
a binary system in which credit is applied only when the completed deliverable is received must be used. Under this system, no credit will be applied if the deliverable has not been
received, regardless of how much time and money have been
spent on the task.

A variety of intermediate crediting methods can be devised
to accommodate situations that do not call for either of these
two extremes. Figure 7-11 shows a partial list of possible crediting methods. The rationale for developing and using these
crediting schemas is to provide project management data as
accurately possible with minimal intrusion into the technical
facets of a particular task.

Although these crediting guidelines seem imprecise—and
they are in fact imprecise at the elemental level—once they
are summarized across WBS levels, the overall progress of the
higher levels of the WBS can be acceptably accurate. The assigned progress percentages do not have to be exceptionally
accurate; in fact, due to the nature of many creativity-based
projects, the accuracy of the assigned progress percentages is

---

Figure 7-11
Progress Reporting for Non-Measurable Activities

- 0%–100% Rule
  - The team will not be credited for progress unless the deliverable is fully delivered.
- 20%–80% Rule
  - The team will get 20% credit for starting the task. Full credit will be applied upon delivery.
- 50%–50% Rule
  - The team will be credited for half of the deliverable upon starting and half upon delivery.
- 30%–30%–40% Rule
  - Not Started: Team will be credited for 0%
  - Just Started: Team will be credited for 30%
  - In Progress: Team will be credited for 60%
  - Completed: Team will be credited for 100%

---

normally somewhat low. Again, notwithstanding the inaccuracy at the lowest level, once the earned values are rolled up to the project level, the accuracy is acceptable if there are no overt biases in determining the elemental earned value.

The value that is earned for each WBS element can be determined by summing the progress made in each of the tasks that must be performed to deliver the WBS element at hand. Figure 7-12 shows the procedure for establishing an earned value system for a deliverable element. The first step in this process is to formulate a list of values during the planning stages of the project. Then, at each reporting milestone, the progress credited to each of the constituents, using any of the crediting methods described earlier, is determined. Total earned value will be the sum of the products of the value amounts and credited progress.

Figures 7-13 through 7-15 show the development of earned value for a segment of a website development project. Figure 7-13 shows a listing of the values that were defined during the planning stages by the stakeholders for this project. The value list can be a compilation of the distribution of either cost or effort among the activities of the element being evaluated.

Figure 7-12
Earned Value

- During planning stage of project
  –Divide the work into discrete components
  –Assign cost to each component
  –Agree on earned value payment
- During execution stage of project
  –Determine progress on each component
  –Calculate earned value

Figure 7-13
Sample Earned Value (website development value list)

Activity Description	Value
• Requirements	10%
• Design	20%
• Develop modules	30%
• Test modules	20%
• Perform integration test	5%
• Document and train	15%
Total deliverables	**100%**

The team's progress in achieving the goals of the element in question is indicated by the total earned value. This progress is determined by summing the credits earned by each of the constituent activities, toward the deliverable, as shown in Figure 7-14. Accordingly, Figure 7-15 shows a computation of the value earned for the deliverable element.

Using the earned value technique at any point during the life of the project, the amount of progress can be determined by summarizing the earned value of lower-level components along the WBS structure. The earned value for the project can be computed by determining the percentage of earned value for each of the constituent components at the lower levels of the WBS.

Figure 7-14
Sample Earned Value (website development reported delivery)

Item	Amount Delivered
• Requirements	100%
• Design	85%
• Develop modules	80%
• Test modules	10%
• Perform integration test	0%
• Document and train	0%
Total progress	**?%**

Figure 7-15
Sample Earned Value (website development recommended payment)

Activity	Value	Delivered	Earned
• Requirements	10%	100%	10
• Design	20%	85%	17
• Develop modules	30%	80%	24
• Test modules	20%	10%	02
• Perform integration test	5%	0%	00
• Document and train	15%	0%	00
Total earned	**100%**	**?**	**53%**

During the early stages of the project, and for small projects, this process involves only a few elements at the first one or two levels. For fully developed projects, the process would involve a very large set of all of the lower-level components of the project, extending to levels 4, 5, and even lower, of the WBS.

Some project managers choose to use a more extensive schema for earned value. This schema is fundamentally based on four terms. These terms, and the resulting predictive indices, are calculated or refreshed at evaluation milestones of the project.

The four terms are:

- PV—What was planned to be done

- AC—What was spent

- EV—What was done

- BAC—Budget at Completion, the amount budgeted for the entire project.

Then, the following series of evaluative and predictive ratios is used to assess the project's current state and to predict its future direction:

- EV-AC = CV, Cost Variance—the amount of cost overrun or underrun

- EV-PV = SV, Schedule Variance—the schedule overrun or underrun in $

- EV/AC = CPI, Cost Performance Index—normalized cost overrun or underrun

- EV/PV = SPI, Schedule Performance Index—normalized schedule overrun or underrun

- BAC/CPI = EAC, Estimate at Completion—updated estimate of total project cost

- BAC-EAC = VAC, Variance at Completion—amount of overrun or underrun at delivery

- (BAC-PV)/CP I= ETC, Estimate to Complete—funds needed to complete the project.

PRODUCTIVITY

The estimate of the cost of an activity, or a project, is based on average or anticipated attributes of the deliverable. This estimate can be refined and updated once it becomes clear who will perform the tasks and what their skill levels are.

The term "productivity" usually is associated with concepts such as spending less money, taking less time, using less effort, and ultimately creating more output with less input (see Figure 7-16). Client factors, such as the specificity of the project objectives, clarity of project plan, and availability of tools, particularly with respect to individual assignments, also affect the team's productivity (see Figure 7-17). In addition, productivity is affected by the characteristics of the project team, such as personal pride, attitude, competency, the motivation to learn, and the desire to excel (see Figure 7-18).

Productivity also is affected by the frequency of unexpected and unexplained changes to the project and the presence of a formalized scope change policy. Productivity depends on the environment created by organizational policies and proce-

---

Figure 7-16
Productivity

- Spend less money
- Take less time
- Use less effort
- Improve quality
- Create less waste
- Reduce rework volume
- Create more output with less input

Figure 7-17
Client Factors That Affect Productivity

- Specificity of project objectives
- Clarity of project plan
- Availability of tools
- Frequency of scope changes
- Formalized scope change policy
- Organizational policies

Figure 7-18
Team Factors That Affect Productivity

- Personal pride
- Attitude
- Competency
- Motivation to learn
- Desire to excel
- Organizational culture
- Type of contract

---

dures with respect to innovation, efficiency, and reward. Finally, experience has shown that the productivity of the contractor's team is additionally affected by the type of the contract.

Strategies that improve workforce productivity include assigning the correct specialty and the correct competency level to each task. Proper assignment of labor will greatly enhance team morale, and verification of such assignment should be an integral part of project progress monitoring.

Sometimes, particularly in projects that involve lengthy or highly repeatable tasks, productivity is expressed by a learning curve. The premise in the concept of a learning curve is that if a task is performed repeatedly, it will take less time to perform that particular task the more frequently it is performed. As an example, designing a web page might take 120 minutes for someone who is doing it for the first time. But, as the same person designs similar pages, each repetition will take a little less time, so that the thirtieth page can be done in, perhaps, 100 minutes.

The extent to which this improvement occurs is determined from plotting task time vs. number of repetitions, otherwise known as the learning curve. Because the learning curve usually is plotted on a log-log scale, a line on that scale will characterize the learning curve; it is therefore called the learning curve even though the most common way of visualizing it is in a linear fashion.

Figure 7-19 shows three separate lines (curves) indicating the rate of productivity improvement for three different operations. This figure shows that after 32 repetitions, one operation gains a 10 percent reduction in performance time, while another gains a 30 percent reduction. For lengthy projects that include highly repetitive tasks, the effect of the learning curve on project cost and duration performance should be considered.

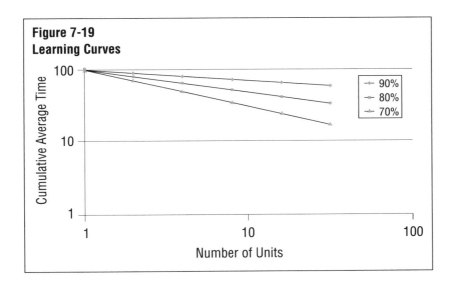

Figure 7-19
Learning Curves

The project manager's effectiveness in dealing with the implementation issues of the project depends heavily on timely and accurate data that describe the progress of crafting, building, and creating the various project components. A good monitoring system should keep the project manager informed of the expenditures and achievements that are associated with the project deliverable. These tasks must be conducted as quickly, accurately, and regularly as possible.

The data to be collected will focus on attributes of the resources, amount of resources, and the project elements on which these resources were spent. Additionally, a logical and proactive monitoring system will highlight the rate of attainment of elemental objectives, particularly in comparison with the anticipated rate of achieving the goals and objectives.

8 Change Management

Cost-schedule management, also known as integrated change management, is the process used during project execution to minimize the cost of the project while maintaining acceptable levels for its duration, quality, and scope of the deliverables. Project information that would form the basis of a progress monitoring and cost-schedule management system include detailed descriptions of client objectives, project requirements, project charter, quality expectations, resource constraints, funding structure, acceptance test details, administrative milestones, and the anticipated delivery date.

The cost-schedule management process should not be treated as separate from the estimating, scheduling, and budgeting processes. Rather, it should be treated as the integrated principal component of a process that is composed of the revolving phases of developing the estimate for cost and duration, establishing the budget, managing the inevitable changes to the project, and making modifications to the estimate and schedule.

If the final, definitive budget is established from an early inaccurate estimate, the project stakeholders must be sensitive to the precision limitations of those estimates. In other words, the project estimate should be treated as a living document and updated as frequently as possible. Therefore, it is reasonable to expect that the estimate of the total cost of the project might vary with every estimate update, although a change in estimate will not necessarily trigger a change in budget.

Even if the estimate of costs were reasonably accurate based on the detailed information available at the time of the early estimates, it is very likely that implementation costs will not match the planned costs due to unexpected changes in client requirements, design philosophy, scope, and project environment. Thus, the data collected during the progress monitoring process will be used to quantify the impact of the project changes on the general direction of the project's overall performance.

The cost-schedule management process is most effective when it is formalized and integrated with the organization's project management policies and procedures. A formalized cost-schedule management process will ensure that all project personnel, in all projects, will follow a specific set of established procedures. A formal management structure will have the added advantage of keeping all the project stakeholders involved in, or at least informed of, the project's performance status, thereby contributing to team spirit and good morale.

It bears repeating that the most effective cost management system is one that ensures consultation with the stakeholders in all triple-constraint tradeoff decisions, and one that facilitates a full and prompt dissemination of the subsequent disposition of each change request to project personnel.

The objectives of the cost-schedule management process are to track progress, compare actual values to planned values, analyze the impact of variances, and make adjustments in light of these variances. Additionally, determination of the variances between planned and actual values should not narrowly focus on the total project; rather, it should span all individual elements of the WBS.

The current value or variance of individual component resource expenditure and costs, as well as those for the total project, should always be at the disposal of the project stakeholders. Interpretation of the progress data from the current project will be performed in light of historical data from previous projects or benchmarking data from other projects within the same industry. These interpretations must be repeated or refreshed on a regular basis and as part of the inevitable scope changes throughout the life of the project.

The impact of each change must be evaluated in terms of scope, cost, schedule, and resource demand. It would be unrealistic to expect good planning to eliminate all unexpected events. On the other hand, when the project is carefully planned, it is logical to expect a reduction of the magnitude and impact of project changes brought on by unexpected events.

Whereas a project with casually evolving plans will contain many unexpected changes, a well-planned project should have significantly fewer unexpected events, and the consequences will be less dramatic. It is therefore essential that the project manager conduct careful early planning to minimize the frequency and impact of project changes.

The next step in change management, which includes both cost and schedule management, is to determine whether or not the performance variances and trends are significant. If variances are significant, an adjustment of the triple constraints must be considered. This adjustment could be simply a change to the budget value alone. Alternately, in response to these new developments in project environment, the adjustment could involve a change to the values of all triple constraints.

The basic administrative structure of a typical cost management system will include a change management board, a configuration management board, a change request form, and a change log. The change management board and configuration management board review the changes from a project management viewpoint and from a technological standpoint, respectively.

The change management board normally is composed of the project manger, the client liaison, client technical personnel, project personnel, and a contract officer if the project is an external project. The change management board is charged with defining and handling project change requests. Then, during the implementation phase, the board ensures compliance with these established processes and procedures. The primary focus of this board is to assess the impact of change on the triple constraints of the project.

The configuration management board normally is composed of all the technical specialties represented in the project deliverable, the client representative, and project management personnel. This board is charged with monitoring and documenting the functional and physical characteristics of the components of the deliverable, as defined in the original project documents. The configuration management board is further charged with managing the changes to these characteristics, optimizing the effects of changes, and verifying conformance of the attributes of the deliverable with the client's evolving specifications.

As an example, the configuration board would be concerned with the impact of these changes on the input/output structure of other modules, processing speed, maintenance complications, database duplication, and system complexity. On the other hand, the change management board would review, in light of the client's current expectations, the impact that a change in a software module might have on the delivery date and on the total cost of the project.

Procedural consistency in data collection and reporting will encourage the stakeholder to review changes, thus preventing ad-hoc implementation of changes. Figures 8-1 and 8-2 show a sample change request form and a typical format for the change management log, respectively. The change request form is the prescribed mechanism for requesting, approving, and announcing project changes. The change log is a historical account of the evolutionary history for scope, configuration, cost, and schedule.

Essential in the cost-schedule management process is maintaining the delicate balance between providing a timely and complete flow of information to those who need a lot of infor-

Figure 8-1
Change Request Form

- Purpose
  - Standardize change request information
- Common elements
  - Name of requester
  - Requester's organization
  - Date of request
  - Description
  - Current status
  - Action requested
  - Change request number
  - Impact/benefit of change

Figure 8-2
Change Management Log

- Purpose
  - To provide a documented record of the change requests received during the project
- Common elements
  - Name of requester
  - Requester's organization
  - Date of request
  - Description
  - Current status
  - Action requested
  - Change request number
  - Impact/benefit of change

mation, while not overwhelming those who do not need to receive all the information. As each report is designed, defined, and distributed, special attention must be paid to the rationale used to determine which particular report is being sent to a particular individual. The expected response from the recipient of that report should also be defined in detail.

The cost-schedule management process need not be elaborate if the project is very small or if it involves only three or four people, although the project cost-schedule management system needs to be formalized nonetheless.

The necessary data and the essential tools of cost-schedule management activities include the current and updated work breakdown structure, cash flow constraints, details of current estimates of time and duration, budgets, timely progress reports, and accurate change reports. Additionally, it would be exceptionally helpful if the change management system were assisted by project management software that is responsive to the specific needs of that particular project.

Project management should never allow the shortcomings and constraints of the project management software package to handicap the change management process. Common solutions for overcoming shortcomings of the standard packages include opting for an add-on to the package or augmenting the software with accounting software such as a spreadsheet or a database package. Of course, selecting a different software package should always be an option.

Experienced project managers are fully aware that treating the budget as an immovable object does not prevent project cost and schedule variations; it simply discourages good record keeping and makes unavailable the data that might have isolated and explained the very likely future cost overruns. When the variance between the current and forecasted cost and duration values exceed the threshold set by the project manager, the project manger should request that the budget be adjusted to the then-current value of the estimate.

Understandably, some project environments preclude this process. In such organizations, project managers tend to add contingency buffers to the early estimates to mitigate the impact of future changes. In very rare cases, project managers do not explicitly show these buffers as such; they simply report the buffer-modified estimate as the definitive estimate. This practice is not recommended because it distorts the historical data collection that is necessary for improving future estimates.

During the project's implementation phase, the project manager will be placed in situations in which he or she must make tradeoffs among the triple constraints of the project. The process of making tradeoffs will be consistent if the project manager, in concert with the stakeholders, has determined the ranking of the triple constraints.

Making such a ranking is very difficult for the stakeholders because they often hold all of the triple constraints as important and somewhat unchangeable. However, it is imperative to determine priorities when faced with choices between, for example, cost and schedule. Put another way, at least one of the triple constraints should be modifiable and forgiving.

CAUSES OF CHANGE

The mission of a change management system is not to control the costs and schedule at the original estimate level, which may or may not have been accurate. The change management process should be designed to manage the inevitable changes to the project with the least combined impact on the triple constraints of cost, schedule, and scope.

Innumerable circumstances can change the project environment or its constraints. However, the circumstances causing change, or the sources of project changes, can be grouped under the major categories shown in Figure 8-3.

Figure 8-3
Reasons for Change

- Changes in client's needs
- Unexpected site conditions and environmental attributes
- Evolution in design philosophy or prevailing technology
- Errors in
  - Design
  - Estimate
  - Schedule
  - Implementation

The first category of changes includes those generated by the client. The client may not have articulated the project objectives correctly or accurately at the inception of the project, and thus midway into its completion, the client may sharpen or modify the focus on the objectives. Such restatements of the project objectives can be implemented without any appreciable effects on project plans, although usually they do affect the baseline plan and cause delivery disruptions.

Client revisions to the requirements can be technical in nature, or they might restate the time, cost, or resource constraints of the project. In turn, time and resource constraints might set new delivery dates, new cash flow patterns, or modified restrictions on overall project expenditures.

Unexpected and unplanned project conditions include items such as changes in operating system, hardware characteristics, environmental platforms, environmental conditions, and occurrences such as strikes, tornados, snow storms, etc. It goes without saying that unexpected events never can be prevented, and their impact cannot be totally eliminated. However, the impact of unexpected events will be minimized in projects that include a comprehensive risk management plan that is fully integrated with the planning process for cost, schedule, and scope. Optimistic project managers hold the belief that a certain number of welcomed and positive unplanned events also are possible.

The occurrence of major evolutions of design philosophy is somewhat frequent in projects that depend on new technology. In projects that are highly dependent on cutting-edge innovations, the design team often will suggest a new design for the deliverables midstream into the project and in light of the current developments in that discipline.

As much as these innovations are welcome in the deliverable, their introduction into the project plan sometimes will have a negative effect on the cost and schedule of the project. Normally, the cost of remedial actions necessary to deal with the changes in circumstances can easily be attributable to the client and will become part of the new budget for the project.

A variation of the change in design philosophy can also occur when the project design team discovers a flaw in the basic design of the project. Depending on the character of this design flaw, corrective measures and product restructuring will affect the cost and schedule of the project. The cost of recovery for this category of events is borne by the contractor if the contractor was responsible for the design, and by the owner if the design was performed by the client or by a third-party designer.

In most projects, there is an ongoing debate as to whether a design change was the result of an infusion of new technology or simply a bug-fixer. This kind of debate does not occur for internal projects—at least not in the same intensity—primarily because the client is responsible for cost overruns regardless of how they happen. Notwithstanding, the separation of the cause of overruns can be used as a mechanism for judging the internal project manager's performance.

Finally, the cost of a project and the delivery schedule may have to be modified to account for implementation errors, such as substandard equipment, low quality components, or excessive error rate for a software component. In the case of external projects, if the client participates in developing the project implementation activities, then the cost of recovery must be shared between the client and the contractor.

If the contract is of the cost-plus type, determining the allocation of these additional costs might become very delicate and complex depending on the extent to which the client orchestrated the contractor's activities. However, if the project is an external fixed-price project, the contractor may need to absorb the cost of recovery from implementation errors. By contrast, if the project is internal, the client will absorb the cost increase for this last category of items as a matter of sponsorship.

Because of the complicated backdrop of contractual issues, when a change is observed in the performance or the objective of an external project, the first issue to be resolved between the client and contractor is to which one of the above categories the new change will rightly belong. The answer will determine who will absorb the resulting cost variances. This debate forms the basis for much client-contractor litigation.

FEED FORWARD

There is no question that some of the data that are collected by the cost-schedule management system will benefit future projects by establishing trends, baselines, and benchmarks. However, detailed cost reporting data also offer substantial benefits for the performance of the current project. These benefits are observed primarily during the status meetings that deal with project change deliberations; detailed progress data will facilitate a more informed decision-making atmosphere. Additionally, in larger projects, data from earlier stages can be used to assist with managing the later stages of the project.

Having a formalized change management process in place makes it possible to fine-tune the estimates of components that will be developed during the later stages of the project on the basis of the performance of earlier components. Figure 8-4 shows the reported progress for one element of the WBS along with the assumptions for that element. Figure 8-5 shows the forecast values for a similar component that will be implemented during the second half of the project.

Figure 8-4
Simple Schedule Network Forecasting (assumptions)

- Expenditures vary linearly with progress
- Expenditures are uniform throughout activity
- Learning and experience curves do not apply
- Activities are not calendar-dependent
- Activities A1 and A2 are nearly identical
- Activity A1 was just finished
- Activity A2 is scheduled

Figure 8-5
Simple Forecasting

- Activity A1 was just completed
  - With 82% of the estimated resources
  - At 109% of the estimated time
- The estimate for Activity A2 must be modified to reflect
  - 18% decrease in resources
  - 9% increase in time
  - ?% change in total A2 cost

The benefits of the availability of detailed project data might extend even further. With a sophisticated cost monitoring and management system in place, and using the feed-forward technique, a seasoned project manager would be able to adjust the estimated progress rate of the second half of a component based on the performance of the first half of the same component.

Literature shows that, in most projects, the trends established during the first 15 percent of the project life are expected to continue through the life of the project unless major redirection is applied (Anonymous[2] 1999). Of course, if the project has not implemented a sophisticated progress monitoring system, these trends will largely go undetected.

IMPACT OF SCHEDULE ON COST

During the project's early planning stages, the cost estimate is predicated on certain assumptions about the pace of the project and about the scope and quality of characteristics of the deliverables. Accordingly, because cost is directly affected by changes in duration and scope, managing the cost always will have to be in concert with managing the scope and schedule. Even when the baseline project scope remains unchanged, changes to the project schedule will result in corresponding changes in the resource expenditure and cost of the project. The midstream project changes may affect the scope, effort, resources, materials, cost, and time.

The traditional and simplest form of conducting projects is sequentially and in phases. This form of project execution minimizes the errors that can be introduced into the project deliverable due to rapid implementation, hasty communication, and workplace congestion. Figure 8-6 shows the traditional project sequencing, which produces the lowest cost of all options, although it takes the longest of all the sequencing options to complete the project.

A typical construction, industrial, or process project will have the following generic phases: preliminary design, detailed design, prototype development, construction, acceptance testing, and turnover. A typical software system development project generally is composed of the following phases: requirement statement, requirement analysis, system design, implementation, unit testing, integration, system testing, and delivery.

Since projects are intended to develop deliverables that must ultimately satisfy a specific business need, there is always a certain amount of pressure on the project manager to finish the project sooner. It is therefore important to be aware of the implications of compressing the project's duration.

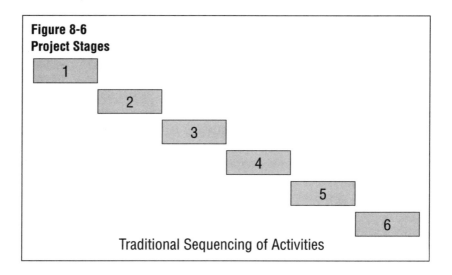

Figure 8-6
Project Stages

Traditional Sequencing of Activities

Experience in construction and industrial projects has shown that there is a threshold beyond which project duration cannot be compressed—normally about 50 percent of the optimum duration. This threshold is commonly referred to as the "crash point." The goal in compressing projects is to compress project duration only to those durations that lie above the crash point.

There are two ways of achieving a shorter duration for the project: by modifying the project scheduling network through sequencing of the various activities and phases, or by shortening the duration of the individual critical path activities of the project.

The network modification is performed after carefully reviewing the network logic and by segmenting bigger activities into smaller ones to achieve a tighter network. If the project duration is compressed by fine-tuning the sequence of the phases, the nature and composition of these components must be changed to accommodate an overlapping execution sequence for the components. Thus, the shorter duration for the project is achieved by breaking the project into as many phases as possible, and starting each phase as soon as possible and not necessarily after the full complement of the logical predecessor phase is completed (see Figure 8-7). This technique is called "fast tracking" in construction projects, "concurrent engineering" in industrial and process projects, and "rapid application development" in software system development projects.

An example of this technique in the construction industry would be to release the design documents in small increments so that construction of the facility can start well before the entire facility is fully designed, rather than wait until all components are designed before beginning the construction (see Figure 8-8). Thus, the constructor will pour the concrete for the foundation while the steel building frame is being designed.

An example of this technique in the software industry is to begin developing individual components as soon as a discrete

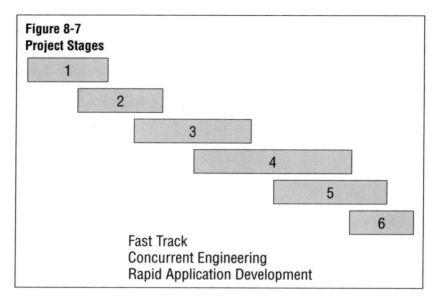

Figure 8-7
Project Stages

Fast Track
Concurrent Engineering
Rapid Application Development

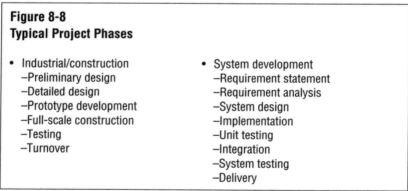

Figure 8-8
Typical Project Phases

- Industrial/construction
  - Preliminary design
  - Detailed design
  - Prototype development
  - Full-scale construction
  - Testing
  - Turnover

- System development
  - Requirement statement
  - Requirement analysis
  - System design
  - Implementation
  - Unit testing
  - Integration
  - System testing
  - Delivery

portion of the requirements is defined. Another example in the software industry is testing individual modules as they are developed, rather than waiting to test all components together when the software development is fully complete. It bears highlighting that testing individual modules one at a time may not be as cost-effective as testing all the modules at the same time, while testing the integrated product. Further, there is an inherent drawback in overlapping phases that are logically serial.

When such phases overlap, the resource intensity impact, cost impact, and even schedule impact of recovery from errors and reworks are somewhat drastic; this cost increase is commonly referred to as the "cost of errors." Notwithstanding, the incentive to use the method of overlapping phases is that if the project is implemented smoothly, the delivery date is far more attractive. This expectation does not always materialize.

The second means of reducing the project duration will involve compressing the critical path—not by reducing the number of activities in the chain, but rather by compressing selected activities of the critical path. Compressing individual critical path activities would involve adding more shifts or a larger crew size to a given activity to reduce its duration, and hence that of the project.

Activities are selected by prioritizing critical path activities based on the costs associated with compressing an activity, by ranking them according to the risk associated with each activity compression, and by prioritizing these elements based on their impact on schedule. Needless to say, critical path elements will not be considered for compression if the associated costs are prohibitive, risk is too high, or schedule impact is minimal.

Remedial actions can be applied only to those elements and activities that have not yet started, and possibly to some that are underway. If the activity or element whose scope has been changed has been completed before the scope increase, the remedial action is reflected as a new activity. If there is a reduction is scope of an activity that has already been completed, there may not be any change in cost if rework is not necessary.

Decrease of scope should, in general, be applied to tasks that are incomplete or not yet started. The strategies for dealing with midstream project changes might include:

- Accept cost change, no schedule change, no quality change

- Perform incomplete tasks by employing personnel with lower rates, if possible

- Reduce duration for incomplete tasks by altering resources, if possible

- Increase productivity by using experts from within the firm

- Increase productivity by using experts from outside the firm

- Reduce scope, if feasible

- Utilize contingency fund of the project

- Conduct a value engineering review

- Change task assignment to take advantage of the schedule float

- Add people to the project

- Outsource the entire project or a significant portion of it

- Compress the schedule

- Work overtime.

Experience in construction, process, and industrial projects has shown that there is a minimum cost for each task and that this minimum cost will occur when the optimum crew size and optimum shift duration are implemented. Therefore, the original project cost baseline should be derived from the original elemental cost baseline, which in turn was developed using optimum crew size for those tasks.

By extension, the baseline duration should be the optimum duration because this is the pristine baseline. The same holds true for the cost. Then, if performance duration other than the optimum duration is chosen midstream for the project, the effects of such duration compression or expansion on cost can be determined methodically and consistently using a formulation similar to the normalized curve depicted in Figure 8-9. This cost-duration relationship can be applied equally well to individual tasks and the project as a whole.

As the estimate of resources and cost for each element and module of the project is refined with new and updated information, the optimum duration and minimum cost of the project are in turn refined and enhanced. Figure 8-9 shows a generic depiction of the relationship between the effort required for the task, hence the cost, and the duration of implementation of that task.

As a rule of thumb, if the duration of the element is halved, the total effort for the activity will double. In other words, there is always a cost penalty for reducing the elemental duration from what is considered to be the optimum. Reducing the duration of the element by 50 percent from its optimum is somewhat drastic. Normally, clients ask for a 10 percent or 20 percent reduction in duration, assuming that the original duration was optimum.

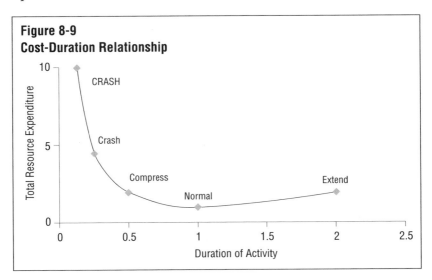

Figure 8-9
Cost-Duration Relationship

Ironically, sometimes it comes as a surprise to the project managers—and to the clients—that when the crew size for an activity is increased to speed the pace of progress, the increased pace is accompanied by a reduction in efficiency. This reduction in efficiency is due to hasty implementation, physical congestion, introduction of new unfamiliar team members to a task that is very time-sensitive, and dramatic increases in communication errors.

Once the number of team members is increased to speed up the project, the lines of communications increase dramatically, along with the probability of miscommunications, duplication of work, and implementation errors. In construction projects, increasing the number of workers will cause physical congestion, which will cause slowdowns and potential safety hazards. In software projects, the detrimental effects of a larger crew are subtler and less visible, but present nonetheless. Notwithstanding these considerations, if the client wishes the project duration to be compressed, that is how the project manager will proceed, although everyone needs to be aware of the fact that schedule compression will carry a cost penalty.

At the other end of the spectrum, if there are resource shortages or cash flow constraints, then the project must be implemented with a smaller size and less-than-optimum crew, in which case it will take longer to finish the project. This deviation from optimum also will increase the total effort of the project, although not to the extent compression would.

If the duration is doubled, the total cost and effort also will double. The reduction in efficiency, which is caused by an increase in duration, is due to penalties involved in more-than-normal start-stop sequences of the processes, reduced team interaction, and deterioration in organizational and individual memory regarding work details and learning curves.

To illustrate the concept of optimum duration, consider an activity that requires five programmers for six days to develop the code for a particular database. If the duration is forced to four days, nine programmers might be required to finish this project. To extend this illustration to an extreme, forcing the duration to three days would require 20 programmers for the same task (see Figure 8-10).

The literature contains extensive historical data regarding the cost penalty for compressing or expanding the schedule network for construction, industrial, and process projects. Therefore, the cost variances for changing project schedules in those industries can be computed reasonably accurately, based on industry-specific data and not necessarily based on generic rates of increase, as shown in Figures 8-9 and 8-10.

If the project is for software and system development and in the absence of satisfactory historical data, the generic ratios stated in these figures can be used as a good first approximation for this relationship. With detailed historical data, discipline-specific mathematical or graphic models can be developed for the optimum duration of the software and system development projects. These models would depict the lowest cost for a specific project conducted in a specific environment.

Some project managers, particularly in software and system development projects, anticipate and react to the possibility of network compression requests by embedding buffers in the original schedule logic. These embedded buffers are created during the planning stages by the inclusion of a lot of sequential activities, to be performed with an understaffed team and using very few parallel activities. Then, once the client makes

---

Figure 8-10
Activity Compression (illustrative example)

Programmers	Duration	Effort
5	6 days	30 worker days
7	5 days	35 worker days
11	4 days	44 worker days
20	3 days	60 worker days

the expected request for duration compression, the project manager announces that some of the serial activities can now be done in parallel. Such a change in plan accommodates the client's wishes, using the proper number of personnel and at minimal additional cost.

This tactic, although proactive and often effective, can be highly explosive. If and when the client becomes aware that the original schedule (and the subsequent compression) was arbitrary, the project manager will lose all credibility and effectiveness in explaining future project variances to the client.

The best policy is to develop a pristine baseline for cost and schedule based on optimum crew size, cost, and duration. Then, as project circumstances such as resource skill, resource availability, and client business needs present themselves, the budget and schedule will be changed, and the client will be apprised accordingly. Notwithstanding, changing durations from optimum value will result in increasing effort and cost, whereas changing the logical relationships of a schedule will not necessarily result in decreasing effort or cost.

PROJECT LIFE-CYCLE COSTS

Enlightened clients tend to keep an eye toward the operational, maintenance, repair, and disposal costs of the project's deliverable. Life-cycle cost analysis and value analysis are two techniques that are used to develop approximations of the total cost of the project. There is some overlap between the life-cycle cost analysis and value analysis.

The purpose of value analysis is to develop a product design strategy that will result in the lowest cost for that particular function or product. The value analysis process, also known as value engineering, will depend on a detailed understanding of the client's needs and desires in terms of the functionality of the deliverable. Then, on the basis of the detailed definition of the desired functions of the product, the value analysis process will produce the specifications for the appropriate hardware or software. A value analysis process might recommend traditional components for the function, or develop a new design to reduce the cost while being responsive to the needs of the client.

Many organizations insist on a value analysis and a life-cycle cost analysis as part of the original cost-estimating phase. In the same fashion that the estimate and the planning data should be treated as living documents, the life-cycle cost analysis and value analysis should be updated frequently during the life of the project. At the very least, life-cycle cost analyses should be revised when the triple constraints go through significant changes or when more details about life-cycle cost issues become available.

The project management life-cycle cost analysis process will incorporate not only the cost of delivering the project, but also the cost of enhancing, maintaining, and ultimately decommissioning it. Operating, decommissioning, and disposal costs must be part of the owner's considerations in cost evaluations during the planning and project selection phases. However, these issues are not always part of the design considerations for the contractor/vendor organizations, unless they are explicitly listed as objectives of the project at hand.

The advantage of using a life-cycle cost analysis is that it puts the overall cost of the deliverable into focus. Sometimes, a product that has the lowest delivery cost may not be the best choice if the overall life-cycle cost of that deliverable is higher than that of other products that are designed for the same set of objectives.

An example of a balance between implementation costs and life-cycle costs is whether to install a pump that is smaller and less expensive than the one originally envisioned. The motivation for this change might be that the smaller pump can be installed faster. However, this change must be made with the full recognition that the operating and repair cost of this pump will be much higher than the one originally designed. Therefore, for comparison purposes, not just the installation costs, but also the sum of the purchase cost and the lifetime operating cost for these two pumps, will need to be compared.

Finally, the project cannot be delivered early without making sacrifices in cost, quality, and scope. A balance is needed between the overall impact of the financial benefits of early delivery of the deliverable and the long-term penalties of a slightly impure deliverable.

An example of such balance in a software project is when the software will lack some of the desired features and may even include some unresolved errors just so that it can be delivered to the client sooner. This expediency might even involve additional costs for more detailed training for operational personnel, debugging the system, and maintaining the system. Accordingly, the cost comparison should be made between the sum of the developmental cost and the lifetime cost for debugging, training, and maintenance.

IMPACT OF PROJECT RISK

For every project, there are possible occurrences that might impact the scope, quality, cost, and schedule. A risk assessment must be conducted as part of the initial planning to determine the possible impact of these occurrences. Once the impact of these occurrences is determined, the project manager will be able to make a decision as to how to deal with such probabilities.

The basic form of risk management is to consider only those risk events that are totally out of the project team's control, such as strikes, floods, tornadoes, and other acts of God. A modified view of risk management would include risks of undesirable occurrences from all sources. This expanded view of risk would include consideration of the impacts of and remedies for cost overrun, schedule delay, physical defects in the deliverable, and performance shortcomings of the deliverable. It is an important point that the latter sets of project attributes are, or should be, under the project team's control.

In developing a risk management plan, the project manager must identify risks in ways that are consistent with corporate policy and with good project management practices. Even more importantly, the same risk identification structure should be used consistently in all projects.

Before and during the occurrence of the risk, the project manager may choose to accept the risk or put provisions in place for dealing with the occurrence of the risk. These provisions could include assigning project personnel to monitor and handle this issue on a contingency basis, or simply developing contingency funds for if and when the risk event materializes. The important issue here is that the project must have a proactive and comprehensive risk management plan in place to mitigate the impact of unexpected events.

One of the means of recognizing the financial impact of, and planning for, risk events is to determine a statistical monetary value for the risk and then somehow incorporate those risk-related expenses into the project estimate. Implementing this simple solution would begin with determining the probability and cost impact of occurrence for each risk event. The product of these two values would be the funds representing the statistical impact of that particular risk.

Once this calculation is conducted for all risk events, the total funds representing the statistical cost impact of all risk events can either be incorporated into the project budget or placed in a separate contingency fund specifically earmarked for dealing with results of risk events (see Figure 8-11). Alternately, depending on the funding structure of the project, risk-related funds might become either part of client reserve or part of project contingency funds.

Figure 8-11
Risk Contingency Funds (simple example)

Risk Event	Probability	Impact	Statistical Impact
Risk 1	10%	$100,000	$10,000
Risk 2	5%	$20,000	$1,000
Risk 3	12%	$80,000	$9,600
Risk 4	15%	$200,000	$30,000
Risk 5	5%	$150,000	$7,500

Total Risk-related Contingency Funds			**$180,000**

Although it is every project manager's dream that the project will follow the plans smoothly and precisely, it is likely that unexpected events will occur. These events usually have a negative impact on the triple constraints of cost, schedule, and scope. Then, the mission of the project manager becomes that of searching for the best compromise in the values of the triple constraints. This objective should not be treated as that of holding the cost, duration, and scope to what was planned many weeks, months, or even years ago, but rather that of providing acceptable values for schedule and scope while minimizing the increase in the project's cost. This process always should be treated as managing the triple constraints, and not necessarily controlling them.

9 Managing Project Knowledge

Improving performance through learning is a common theme to formalized project management (PM) and knowledge management (KM), although KM focuses on knowledge in all areas beyond managing projects. Specifically, knowledge acquisition, development, transfer, and utilization are common functions to both.

PM's focus is on improving project performance through improving the processes associated with the organization's projects as a whole. On the other hand, KM's focus is on improving the efficiency and effectiveness of all recognized formalized disciplines throughout the enterprise. PM can be regarded as an integral part of KM as projects deal with new things that, to be developed, require an understanding of the organization's past and current projects (Cioffi 2002).

In the current business environment, competition is increased because of globalization and free market philosophy. This environment has posed far greater challenges than ever for organizations to meet customer needs. It compels organizations to develop products and services faster, cheaper, and better to retain a competitive advantage in the marketplace.

This competitive advantage can be attained and maintained by exerting significant influence on how organizations practice both PM and KM. Thus, it is important to be aware of all the common aspects of both these disciplines, and how KM practices can enhance PM in fulfilling its time, cost, performance, and customer satisfaction goals.

THE INTERRELATIONSHIP BETWEEN PM AND KM

A project has a definite beginning, definite ending, and several interdependent tasks. Unfamiliarity and uniqueness are often described as characteristics of a project. Formalized project management is concerned with completing a project on time, within budget, and according to the project specifications while satisfying both the customer and project team expectations. Project management is essentially the application of specific procedures, tools, and skills in achieving the client's goals, as reflected in the project objectives.

Knowledge is a resource that increases its value with use. Although the terms "knowledge" and "information" are commonly used interchangeably, they have separate and distinct meanings in the area of knowledge management.

Information is that entity that gives quantitative, or even qualitative, form to our experiences, in the form of language, numbers, pictures, and diagrams. Information allows us to communicate our basic observations and perceptions. On the other hand, knowledge is far more than information, because it includes the meaning and interpretation of the information. Knowledge also includes intangibles such as the tacit knowledge of experienced people—something that is not well articulated but often determines collective organizational competence (Nevis, DiBella, & Gould 1995). Thus, knowledge can be defined as insights derived from information and experience.

Ironically, knowledge will remain dormant, and not very useful, until it is reflected in future actions. KM is the systematic, explicit, and deliberate building, renewal, and application of knowledge to maximize an enterprise's knowledge-related effectiveness and to improve returns from its knowledge assets (Wiig 1993).

The primary focus of KM is to utilize information technology and tools, business processes, best practices, and culture to create and share all categories of knowledge within the organization and to connect those people who possess knowledge to those people who are in need of that knowledge. A well guided and properly practiced KM effort will lead to enhanced organizational performance in all specialty areas. Given the overlap between PM and KM disciplines, a discussion on their similarities is a prerequisite to managing project knowledge.

Goals

PM is concerned with project scope, schedule, cost, and performance of meeting stakeholder expectations. KM, on the other hand, is a deliberate effort to develop knowledge in all specialty areas and share it throughout the enterprise. KM efforts ultimately will lead to better organizational performance in all operational and specialty areas.

Functions

The PM discipline involves planning and controlling the functions and processes that involve projects. PM is concerned with working together in teams, sharing information, sharing knowledge, learning from each other, and collaborating on efforts to improve project performance. Working in teams, learning from each other, and collaborating also are integral parts of KM.

Communication

Effective communication is critical to success for both PM and KM disciplines. Specifically, communication assumes greater importance for large and complex projects, as the number of communication channels is associated with the number of people, disciplines, and agencies involved in a project. With respect to KM, acquiring and developing, storing, sharing, retaining, and utilizing knowledge are core functions of KM, and they all rely on effective communication. While project communications are generally real-time, KM communications occasionally can happen some time after the knowledge has been discovered.

Structure

It is not uncommon to find that organizations that are involved in multiple projects change their organizational structures from functional organizations to pure project or matrix organizations. In some cases, organizations establish PMOs to facilitate this transition through a formal structure.

While PM has significant influence on organization structure, KM's influence is more subtle. It focuses on acquiring, creating, developing, sharing, and utilizing knowledge. Thus, KM encourages organizations to become flat, reducing hierarchy. Additionally, KM can guide organizations toward creating informal structures for communities of practice, social networks, and virtual teams.

Technology

PM uses technology tools (e.g., statistical modeling tools for estimating, project portfolio selection models, risk analysis schemas, PM software) to plan, monitor, analyze, and control project performance. If a full-scale PMO has been established, then organizational project management will use an intranet, the Internet, videoconferencing, knowledge repositories, expert database systems, artificial intelligence tools, and electronic yellow pages to capture tacit and explicit knowledge of individuals in the organization and to integrate with organizational explicit knowledge. Again, the distinction is that KM's application and scope of these tools go well beyond managing projects.

Knowledge

Both KM and PM engage in acquiring, creating, transferring, retaining, sharing, and utilizing knowledge. The PMO plays an important role in accomplishing these knowledge-related activities. It is becoming increasingly evident that organizations need the PMO to improve the overall and consistent performance of projects. While a formal-structure PMO manages PM knowledge, KM uses other organizational entities and other systems and processes for these purposes.

Process

Given that both PM and KM efforts require investment, the organization anticipates tangible results from their efforts. While the size of a project determines the resources and investment needed for a project, investment in a PMO within an organization depends on the goals of project performance excellence set by the organization. Likewise, the specific objectives of the KM system will determine its investment needs.

KM and PM disciplines have their own sets of processes that will require changes to their existing policies and procedures on implementation. To implement PM and KM successfully, organizations need to make changes in policies, practices, and accounting and other procedures, as well as train people at all levels. While PM demands project-based finance- and cost-control mechanisms, KM will facilitate innovative cost-measuring concepts, such as those recognizing the intangible assets represented by intellectual capital.

Change

By definition, projects are new entities, and all new things are associated with change. Successful implementation of projects will lead to changes, such as new organizational processes and products. These changes might in turn trigger changes in marketing and business strategies, in building new facilities, in work functions, and in business-related technologies. Likewise, learning associated with KM will lead to changes in management functions, processes, work functions, and human behavior.

Learning

Conceptually, both PM and KM are associated with learning that results in behavioral change—both individual and organizational. Learning, which is integral to KM, is a key concept in leveraging knowledge. Well-defined learning processes are prerequisites for organizational learning and for accumulating knowledge in organizations. People within an organization play a critical role in creating and sharing knowledge.

Individual learning, a prerequisite to organizational learning, is characterized by thinking, personal experience, needs and motives, interests and values, level of difficulty of the task at hand, and manifestation of behavioral changes (see Figure 9-1). On the other hand, collective thinking and creation of a shared frame of reference characterize organizational learning. Organizational learning is defined as a process by which the organization's knowledge and value base is changed, thus leading to improved problem-solving, which in turn leads to increased capacity for action (Probst & Buchel 1997).

The major distinction between individual learning and organizational learning is that the former normally uses tacit knowledge, while the latter always uses explicit knowledge. Employees may develop optimum processes while performing tasks within the rules of the organization. On the other hand,

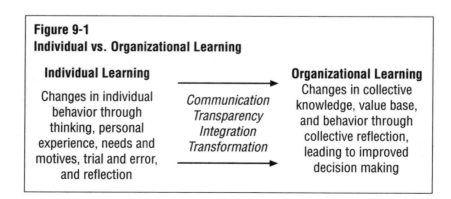

Figure 9-1
Individual vs. Organizational Learning

Individual Learning

Changes in individual behavior through thinking, personal experience, needs and motives, trial and error, and reflection

Communication
Transparency
Integration
Transformation

Organizational Learning

Changes in collective knowledge, value base, and behavior through collective reflection, leading to improved decision making

organizations gain knowledge by documenting these processes and by using these documents as references. Through replicating these processes, organizations acquire additional knowledge, which becomes independent of individuals who developed the original processes.

While individual learning is similar in PM and KM, they adopt different approaches to organizational learning (see Figure 9-2). The PMO formalizes organizational learning for PM through several means and processes with a focus on improving project performance, whereas KM focuses on improving organizational performance by employing technology tools and social networks within an organization.

Practice

Neither the PM nor the KM discipline can be considered new, as evidenced by the fact that they have been recognized by professional societies, industrial organizations, and the academic community. PM has become an integral part of the business

Figure 9-2
Organizational Learning—PM and KM

Project Management	Knowledge Management
Organizational learning is accomplished in project management through a formal structure, known as the project management office (PMO).	Organizational learning is not formal and visible in knowledge management.
Organziational learning through the PMO focuses on improving project performance.	Organizational learning associated with knowledge management is reflected in business practices and policies to enhance organizational performance.

environment, slowly evolving over centuries. Similarly, the social, economic, and technological progress of society is a testimony to KM practices through an age-old tradition of training, education, and social activities.

PMO AND CoP

The PMO's mission is to improve the capabilities of PM in the organization by offering tools, techniques, systems, standards, and relevant knowledge that assist in the effective and efficient execution of projects. The PMO is most appropriate for organizations with multiple projects, locations, contractors, and resources. Poor project performance, and particularly runaway projects, are sometimes the forces behind establishing a PMO.

One of the major functions of the PMO at both the project and enterprise levels is in KM. The PMO is not only about keeping records of what happened in the past, but also about managing future projects better.

At the organizational level, one of the most important functions of the PMO is to instill PM culture in organizations by:

- Developing project management skills and knowledge

- Developing knowledge repositories of project performance and lessons learned

- Improving the maturity of project management.

The establishment of communities of practice (CoP) serves the same function to the KM discipline as the PMO does to PM. Unfortunately, the concept of CoP has not yet been fully developed and formalized. Currently, CoPs are voluntary, formed through individual common interest, expertise, and passion. Given that formal work groups and teams have legitimacy within the organization, these informal groups will cease to exist once these goals are achieved.

In addition to sharing both tacit and explicit knowledge, CoPs offer several other benefits. According to Wenger and Snyder (1999), communities of practice:

- Contribute to strategic direction

- Create new business opportunities

- Solve problems quickly

- Transfer best practices

- Develop professional skills

- Help companies retain talent.

It is highly beneficial for organizations to integrate the CoPs with the PMO to arrive at the most useful outcomes of KM, such as enhanced communication, improved collaboration, and advanced employee skills (Anantatmula 2004).

IMPROVING PM THROUGH KM

PM theory and concepts are organized into different bodies of knowledge, and as such as they are considered independent functions. By comparison, KM is more dynamic and interactive in nature due to continuous transformation of tacit to explicit knowledge. Snider and Nissen (2003) contend that the fluid view of knowledge is at odds with the static view implied by the body of knowledge of professional fields such as PM. However, a dynamic model of continuous learning and improvement is attainable by continuously integrating KM techniques and tools with PM functions.

It is reasonable to expect that the effective integration of KM and PM will result in enhanced collaboration, improved communication, productivity, employee skills, and better decision making. These improvements will be not only for the PM functions, but also for the entire organization, thereby achieving continuous learning and improvement in project performance.

The following KM systems and tools, used throughout the project life cycle, can improve project performance:

- Project selection using knowledge-based decision systems

- RBS development of a project environment, kept current by using up-to-date resource cost information from historical project data and resource database systems

- Project plan and scope development using historical data of projects from knowledge repositories related to project plans and scope definitions

- Accurate and realistic project cost estimation using historical cost and effort estimation and earned value data of past projects

- Project WBS development using standardized WBS packages maintained in database systems

- Realistic and optimum schedule development using historical schedule data and "after action review" information from knowledge repositories

- Resource management based on actual resource usage of similar projects and tasks from database systems

- Risk reduction using available project information and knowledge.

Figure 9-3 presents a dynamic integration model of KM and PM. Simultaneously applying and integrating KM and PM tools will provide updated information and knowledge for managing projects better. These goals will be achieved by reinforcing promising practices and reviewing actions during the project and after its completion.

**Figure 9-3
PM—KM Integration**

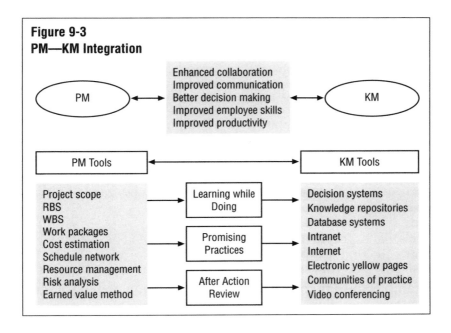

In turn, the project performance data from various segments of the project will feed back into knowledge data repositories and database systems, with the resulting continuous loop providing an opportunity for fluid knowledge flow between PM and KM systems. For example, the project execution phase will provide actual data about resource utilization, individual and collective resource effort required for different tasks, associated costs, and the performance of each resource. In turn, these data will be of immense value in refining RBS and skill levels.

The model suggests dynamic interaction between KM and PM tools, not only at the start and the end of the project but also throughout the project's implementation. It suggests continuous transformation of tacit knowledge into explicit knowledge and vice versa. Some of the KM tools, such as an intranet, video conferencing, and electronic yellow pages of experts, will support the project execution phase by enhancing collaboration and improving communication among the project team members.

Extensive team interaction almost always results in improved employee skills and productivity. These tools also improve team participation and decision making. An intranet can be used to document achievements and lessons learned on a daily basis. Video conferencing tools can be used to tap expertise and knowledge of people who are within the organization but in a different location. Likewise, electronic yellow pages can be used to seek expert advice for all phases of project planning and execution.

A classic example of integrating PM and KM is developing PM software that shifts its traditional focus on quantitative aspects of PM to both qualitative and quantitative aspects. For example, the day-to-day learning and decision making of project team members can be an integral part of PM software.

Ultimately, dynamic project planning based on learning while executing projects is an important result of improving PM performance through KM. One of the most important elements of PM is project integration, which promotes unity of effort in projects by integrating all project-related knowledge. It can be achieved by the dynamic integration model of PM and KM.

Integrating KM and PM tools will have an impact on PM at various levels (see Figure 9-4). All the KM outcomes will have a positive impact at the individual, team, project, PMO, and organizational levels. Together, improved collaboration, communication, employee skills, productivity, and decision making will increase project-related knowledge, which will in turn will benefit overall project performance. Integrating KM and PM is necessary to manage project knowledge effectively and to help organizations improve their project performance.

Figure 9-4
Impact of KM Criteria on Various Areas of PM

Knowledge Management Outcomes	Impact Area for Individual/Team	Impact Area for Project	Impact Area for PMO	Impact Area for Organization
Enhanced Collaboration	–Team Performance –Cooperation –Productivity –Team Dynamics	–Project Scope –Estimation –Schedule –Integration –Execution	–Project Plans –Project Teams –Project Managers –Across Projects –SIG	–PMO –Functions –Units –Divisions
Improved Communication	–Project Specifications –Organization Needs –Integration –Action Plan	–Risk Management –Monitoring and Control –Integration –Conflict Resolution	–Team Performance –PM Selection –Communities –SIG –PM Standards	–Operations –Image –Work Culture
Better Decision Making	–Project Teams –Team Participation	–Project Scope –Estimation –Schedule –Integration –Execution –Project Termination	–Project Plan –Execution –Resource Allocation –Performance –Project Termination	–Project Selection –Strategies –Policies –Growth
Improved Employee Skills	–Innovative Solutions –Accomplishment –Motivation –Team Development	–Resource Allocation –Estimation –Schedule –Integration –Execution	–People Resources –Resource Deployment –Outsourcing –Knowledge Repository –Consulting –Training	–Attraction of Talent –Employee Retention –Employee Morale
Improved Productivity	–Job Satisfaction –Reward –Team Performance –Team Dynamics	–Cost –Schedule –Earned Value –Procurement –Project Performance –Cost-Benefit Analysis	–Promising Practices –Lessons Learned –PM Standards	–Profitability –Investment Potential –Budgeting –Project Finance –Competitive Advantage

Many organizations have come to the conclusion that creating, transferring, and managing knowledge are critical for success. Both PM and KM play a key role in improving organizational performance in delivering products or services better, faster, and cheaper. KM leads to improved communication, improved productivity, better decision making, enhanced collaboration within a project team and across projects, and improved skills of project team members.

Using KM with PM offers several benefits, including better project integration, reduced risk associated with unknown factors, and continuous improvement of project execution. KM also helps distill new processes from previously executed projects.

Bibliography

Anantatmula, V. "Criteria for Measuring Knowledge Management Efforts in Organizations." UMI Dissertation Services (3123064). Ann Arbor, MI: ProQuest, 2004.

Anbari, F. T. *Quantitative Methods for Project Management.* New York: International Institute for Learning, 1997.

Anonymous. *A Guide to the Project Management Body of Knowledge (PMBOK®).* Sylva, NC: Project Management Institute, 2000.

Anonymous. *Parametric Estimating Handbook.* 2d ed. Washington, D.C. : U.S. Department of Defense, Spring 1999.

Anonymous. *Richardson's Plant Cost Estimating Standards.* Mesa, AZ: Richardson, 1998.

Anonymous. *RS Means Construction Reference.* Kingston, MA: RS Means Construction Reference Books, 2000.

Anonymous. *Skills and Knowledge of Cost Engineering.* 4th ed. Morgantown, WV: AACE, September 1999.

Anonymous. *NASA Cost Estimating Handbook.* Washington, D.C.: NASA HQ, 2002.

Baker, J. "Cost/time trade-off analysis for the critical path method: A derivation of the network flow approach." *Journal of the Operational Research Society* 48, no. 12 (December 1997): 1241–1244.

Cioffi, D. *Managing Project Integration.* Vienna, VA: Management Concepts, 2002.

DeNeufville, R., and E. Hani. "Bidding models: Effects on bidders' risk aversion." *ASCE Journal of the Construction Division* 103, no. CO1 (March 1977) 57–70.

Foldes, Stephen, and François Soumis, "PERT and crashing revisited: Mathematical generalizations." *European Journal of Operational Research* 64, no. 2 (January 22, 1993): 286–294.

Garvin, D. *Learning in Action.* Boston, MA: Harvard Business School Press, 2000.

Gates, Marvin. "Bidding Model—A Monte Carlo experiment." *ASCE Journal of the Construction Division* 102, no. 4 (December 1976): 669–680 .

Gates, Marvin. "Review of existing and advanced construction estimating techniques." *Proceedings of 1978 Conference on Construction Estimating and Cost Control Methods.* New York: ASCE Construction Division, 1978.

Gates, Marvin, and Amerigo Scarpa. "Optimum working time." *Transportation Engineering Journal* 103, no. 4 (November 1977): 773–781 .

Gates, Marvin, and Amerigo Scarpa. "Reward-risk ratio." ASCE *Journal of the Construction Division* 100, no. 4 (December 1974): 521–532.

Gould, Frederick E. *Managing the Construction Process: Estimating, Scheduling, and Project Control.* New York: Wiley, 1996.

Gray, C.F., and E.W. Larsen. *Project Management: The Managerial Process.* 2nd ed. New York: McGraw-Hill, 2003.

Hall, E., and J. Johnson. *Integrated Project Management.* Columbus, OH: Prentice Hall, 2003.

Ibbs, C.W., and Y.H. Kwak. *The Benefits of Project Management: Financial and Organizational Rewards to Corporations.* Sylva, NC: PMI® Publications, 1997.

Jandy, G., and K.Tanczos. "Network scheduling limited by special constraint as a function of time cost." *Periodica Polytechnica Transportation Engineering* 15, no. 2 (1987): 35.

Kerr, Richard A. "A system fails at Mars, a spacecraft is lost." *Science* 286 (November 19, 1999): 1457–1459.

Kerzner, H. *Project Management: A Systems Approach to Planning, Scheduling, and Controlling.* 6th ed. New York: John Wiley & Sons, Inc., 1998.

Kerzner, H. *Applied Project Management: Best Practices on Implementation.* New York: John Wiley & Sons, 2000.

Klastorin, T. *Project Management: Tools and Trade-Offs.* New York: John Wiley & Sons, 2004.

Meredith, J., and S.J. Mantel. *Project Management: A Managerial Approach.* 5th ed. New York: John Wiley & Sons, 2003.

Michaels, Jack V., and William P. Wood. *Design to Cost.* New York: John Wiley & Sons, 1989.

Navarrete, Pablo. *Planning, Estimating, and Control of Chemical Construction Projects.* New York: Marcel Dekker, Inc., 1995.

Nevis, E., A. DiBella, and J. Gould. "Understanding organizations as learning systems." *MIT Sloan Management Review* 1995, 36, no. 2 (Winter): 73–86.

Ostwald, Phillip F. *Engineering Cost Estimating.* 3rd ed. Englewood Cliffs, NJ: Prentice Hall, 1991.

Probst, G. and B. Buchel. *Organizational Learning: The Competitive Advantage of the Future.* London: Prentice Hall, 1997.

Pulat, P., and S. Horn. "Time-resource tradeoff problem." *IEEE Transactions on Engineering Management* 43, no. 4 (November 1996): 411–416.

Rad, P.F. "Deliverable-oriented work breakdown structure." *AACE Cost Engineering* 40, no. 12 (December 1999): 35–39.

Rad, P.F. *Project Estimating and Cost Management.* Vienna, VA: Management Concepts, 2002.

Rad, P.F., and D. Cioffi. "Work and resource breakdown structures for formalized bottom-up estimating." *Cost Engineering* 46, no. 2 (February 2004): 31–37.

Rad, P.F., and G. Levin. *Advanced Project Management Office.* Boca Raton, FL: CRC Press, 2002.

Remer, D.S., and C. Wong. "Cost scale UP factors for airport construction." *Cost Engineering* 38, no. 2 (February 1996): 24–26.

Schlick, Haim. "Schedule and resources of fast track renovation work." *ASCE Journal of the Construction Division* 107, no. 4 (December 1981): 626.

Sipos, Andrew. "Project time-cost optimization with the purchase time method." *Cost Engineering* 40, no. 7 (July 1998): 22.

Snider, K.F., and E. Nissen. "Beyond the body of knowledge: A knowledge-flow approach to project management theory and practice." *Project Management Journal* 34, no. 2 (June 2003): 4.

Stephen, Soumis, and François Foldes. "PERT and crashing revisited: Mathematical generalizations." *European Journal of Operational Research* 64, no. 2 (January 1993): 65.

Stewart, Rodney D, Richard M. Wyskida, and James D. Johannes. *Cost Estimator's Reference Manual.* 2nd ed. New York: John Wiley & Sons, 1991.

Tahn, Erenguc, and E. Selcuk. "Resource constrained project scheduling problem with multiple crashable, a heuristic procedure." *European Journal of Operational Research* 107, no. 2 (June 1998): 250–259.

Verzuh, E. *The Fast Forward MBA in Project Management.* New York: John Wiley & Sons, 1999.

Vigder, M.R., and A.W. Kark. *Software Cost Estimation and Control.* Ottawa, Ont.: National Research Council of Canada, February 1994.

Vrat, Prem, and Charoen Khenakrairut. "Goal programming model for project crashing with piecewise linear time-cost trade-off." *Engineering Costs and Production Economics* 10, no. 2 (June 1986): 46.

Wenger, E., and W. Snyder. "Communities of practice: the organizational frontier." *Harvard Business Review* 78, no. 1 (January–February 2000): 139–145.

Wiig, K. *Knowledge Management Foundations: Thinking About Thinking—How People and Organizations Create, Represent, and Use Knowledge.* Arlington, TX: Schema Press, 1993.

Index

external and usable size, 108
external projects
  advantages and
    disadvantages, 163–164
  allowance, 180–181
  bids, 169, 176–178
  contingency, 181–182
  contracts, 168–173
  cost plus, 170–173
  direct costs, 179
  fixed price, 169–171
  focused design
    specifications, 166
  functional specifications, 166
  generic performance
    specifications, 166
  importance of, 13
  indirect costs, 179–180
  lump sum, 169–171
  modifiers, 172–173
  overhead, 180
  product specifications, 166
  profit margin, 177
  project audit, 182–184
  project costs, 178–182
  project termination types,
    184
  response to specifications,
    173–176
  schedule termination, 184
  scope creep, 168
  specifications, 164–168
  time and material, 170–172
  unit price, 171–172

F

failed projects, 4
fast tracking, 219
feasibility cost estimate, 115
feed forward, 28, 216–217

final cost estimate, 115
financial characteristics,
  quantitative organizational
  indices, 14
finish-finish relationship (FF),
  144
fixed price contract, 169–171
focused design specifications,
  166
frame material, 119
functional specifications, 166
function points, 120
functions, 233

G

generic performance
  specifications, 166
goals, 233
ground conditions, 119
guaranteed maximum, 173

H

hardware, 31
hardware specifications, 5–6
historical data, 102, 107, 114

I

implementation, 218
implementation cost, 120
implementation errors, 106, 215
indirect costs, 13, 179–180
industry type, 108
information *versus* knowledge,
  232
integration, 30, 218
intensity, of resource, 111
intermediate milestones, 9